SpringerWienNewYork

Roger Riewe (Ed.)

space
condition

International Architecture Symposium

SpringerWienNewYork

steirischerherbst

International
Architecture
Symposium
Graz University of
Technology
25.10. 2002

Content space

condition

PREFACE

All over the world, architectural projects, whether built or not-implemented, are published in glossy brochures and monographs and are thereby presented to an interested specialist audience. Any discussion of this published material only takes place indirectly (if at all) in that, through new projects, there is an element of reaction to those published. However, there is rarely an immediate discussion. Although it would be very important, as it would clarify and sharpen up both positions and attitudes. This non-discussion surely cannot be put down to laziness or a 'keep-out' attitude in an ivory tower, but might rather be caused by the attitude of the print media. They are either too slow and inert or do not have enough space to give room to and support highly complex architectural discussions. Therefore, in a time of new media and real-time communication, it becomes clear that face to face meetings are of paramount importance, not only for reasons of getting to know each other but mainly for reasons of a direct and immediate

exchange, offering the chance to react to
participants and to what was said, so that the
discussion can be deeper and more thorough. These
face to face meetings seem to be the only chance to
deal with complex architectural questions properly.
Therefore, symposia, especially the ones that have a
certain structure in terms of contents and topic, are
enormously important

Preface

Roger Riewe

After the "Latent Utopias" exhibition, organised by steirischer herbst, had been given a fixed date, upon agreement with Peter Oswald, the director of steirischer herbst, and the exhibition curators Zaha Hadid and Patrik Schumacher, I embarked on the organisation of the symposium in parallel with the exhibition. My principal approach for the symposium was neither to have the teams exhibited in "Latent Utopias" being presented and explained by theorists, nor to oblige the exhibited teams to make statements of principle and positioning. Rather, we wanted theorists of architecture and critics to point out and discuss topical themes of contemporary architecture in a round-table discussion. Thus the exhibition mentioned would be embedded in a wider context, and implicit topics would be rendered accessible to the interested specialist audience through the present publication.

SPACE CONDITION

ARCHITECTURE CONDITIONS SPACE.

Space, public space in particular, is subject to continuous change. What is the role of architecture in this context? Can architecture co-determine this change or is it limited to mere reaction? Will there be a final competition between everyday and one-off events, even though they depend on one another?

Architectural conditioning of public space contributes to an increase of cultural values. Can individual projects such as Guggenheim Bilbao

change a region? Is it new strategies or changes of paradigms that will contribute to the conditioning of space? In the coming age of mass customisation, the architectural symposium "space condition" was supposed to embark on the search for new architectures.

To what extent are space-conditioning aspects dependent on time, or should they rather be seen as location-specific? What synergies can we expect between global themes and local, everyday impressions? Global versus local, or is there indeed a glocal?

Architecture in a time in which both ideologies and manifestos are missing, in a time of "political correctness": what can we expect of the architecture of the future? New strategies, or even a new kind of radicalism?

Does the approach of utopia not, at the same time, hold a certain degree of failure? Hence there were numerous questions that were supposed to be addressed within "space condition". The clarifying process promised to be thrilling, especially with the focus on the group of those who had been exhibited in "Latent Utopias".

Thus the question was raised as to which theorists and critics of architecture should be invited for the discussion of the complex of topics with the exhibited teams.

After extended reflections and agreements as far as contents and dates were concerned, the circle of critics was fixed with Bart Lootsma (NL), Neil Leach (GB), Aaron Betsky (NL), Kari Jormakka (FIN), Xavier Costa (ESP) and Michael Speaks (USA), who on one single day (this is how much time we gave ourselves) should discuss the above-mentioned topics with AA-Design research Lab (GB), angèli graham pfenninger scholl architecture (CH), Asymptote (USA), branson coates architecture (GB), dECOi (F), Foreign Office Architects (GB), Greg Lynn FORM (USA), Zaha Hadid Architects (GB), Kolatan / Mac Donald Studio (USA), Ross Lovegrove (GB), MVRDV (NL), ocean D (GB), ocean NORTH (FIN), Pichler & Traupmann (A), propeller z (A), Sadar Vugar Arhitekti/The Designers Republic (SL/GB), servo (S/USA), Softroom (GB), the next ENTERprise (A), UN Studio (NL) and veech.media.architecture (A).

Graz University of Technology made the venue available. As we were expecting a large number of visitors, the symposium was housed in three different locations within the university, which were very close to each other. Location A was the Aula, location B Lecture Hall 2 and location C Lecture Hall 1. With this spatial layout, we made a virtue of necessity, by occupying a panel in each location A and B which would simultaneously communicate via video conference. The whole discussion could be followed in all three locations. Thereby it was possible to give all invited guests the floor in the short time available, with the "Latent Utopias" exhibition opening on the same day, and there was enough room for the audience too.

The substantial support given by steirischer herbst and the Graz University of Technology made this symposium possible. However, I was also very lucky to be able to work with an excellent team, in particular the staff of my institute.

Due to the fact that we do not continuously organise symposia, especially of this kind, we were all very excited.

Guests were invited, flights booked and rebooked, hotel rooms reserved, the framework programme had to be agreed with steirischer herbst, audio-visual technology conceived. Invitations printed, a homepage installed, catering plus tent ordered. So one question remained, how many guests would come and could we handle it if a lot of people turned up?

The first guests arrived on the evening of October 24th, 2002. Several busses from Slovenia and excursions from Vienna registered.

On the morning of October 25th, 2002, at 8:30 am the first people started arriving at Graz University of Technology. The stream of visitors became denser and denser. The invited architects and critics turned up, one after another.

At 9:00 am not all of the panel participants had been spotted.

9:15, 15 minutes late: raise the curtain!

Welcome Address

Erich Hödl
Peter Oswald
Roger Riewe

ERICH HÖDL

Ladies and Gentlemen, welcome to the Graz University of Technology. We are very proud to have this important symposium on space condition here at our institution. A special welcome to all experts in architecture and architectural theory, who come from many countries and who, I would say, are among the most prominent architects of the world. They are part of the avant-garde. It is evident, that such an international symposium is beyond the means of the university alone, therefore I would like to warmly thank the director of the steirischer herbst, Peter Oswald, for the excellent cooperation which has already become a tradition in the last few years. As you know, there is today a correlated exhibition on "Latent Utopias", which will be opened tonight, I think this is a very strong link to this symposium.

Ladies and Gentlemen, the subject of this symposium is undoubtedly an important one. In these rapidly changing times, the space in which we live our worldly lives is intimately linked to the quality of life, the space conditions many aspects of our quality of life. The public space in particular, is an important aspect of the space question. I would say, it is of foremost importance. We no longer have some fixed and overall accepted ideology in architecture nor do we have manifestos which are accepted.

This proves again, that we live in a post modern time and for this reason, we must have an open discussion concerning many aspects of our society, but certainly including architecture. For this reason, I think the discussion has to be organised very openly and I'd like to take this

Erich Hödl

Peter Oswald

opportunity to thank Roger Riewe, who has organised this conference as a real forum, a discussion forum where you, the participant, can choose the theme and also the individuals with whom you want to discuss openly and have personal contact with. I think, to have this organisation in several rooms here is also a kind of space organisation in itself. I would say, this is an experimental discussion and experimental discussions are needed if you no longer have an ideology or a manifesto, which had tradition in architecture. This symposium is organised in an institution, which has quite a long tradition in architecture and I say that we also have many prominent architects, at least in the German speaking countries, coming out of the Graz University of Technology. We, as an institution, have several faculties in engineering and natural science and I say, that architecture is one of the diamonds at this university. A year ago we had an international peer review evaluation of our faculty of architecture and the results were very inspiring, the results had also given some push to rethinking the organisation, concerning learning, teaching and research. We are on a good path to advancing this faculty in a tradition, which has been accepted here for a long time and has also led to the reputation of this faculty. We have about 1,700 students at the faculty and this makes it one of the largest faculties at our university. The restructuring of a faculty and in this case of architecture is also bound to the new university law in Austria. We are going into a period of more autonomy and more responsibility to develop our profile and I think, the faculty of architecture has been doing quite well since last year, especially after this evaluation. I therefore thank the entire staff of the architectural faculty and again Roger Riewe for having organised this conference. I hope that this conference is also input for our rethinking at the university but certainly it goes beyond our institution, and as we have so many international participants I think this is an opportunity to include our institution in an international discussion on space. But as space is a very general theme, many aspects of architecture are involved in this subject. For this conference I wish you fruitful discussions, especially creative discussions and I think, it should also be in such a spirit that the openness of universities is demonstrated, because architecture and many other disciplines are closely linked to society as a whole and giving a positive input to the development and the betterment of society must also be an aim of architecture. Thank you for coming and I wish you a good symposium. Thank you.

PETER OSWALD

Thank you Erich Hödl. Ladies and Gentlemen. Our festival steirischer herbst 2002 focuses on radical experiment within contemporary architecture. The exhibition "Latent Utopias" presents current architectural experiments with radically new concepts of space. This exhibition is curated by Zaha Hadid and Patrik Schumacher and welcome to Brigitte Felderer, who brought the three of us together years ago and I am very happy about this coincidence. Yah, the visitors will be able to move through a series of unfamiliar spaces. There is a great diversity of experiences, installations range from abstract, three dimensional compositions to models of ongoing projects, from unfamiliar furniture to semi-abstract inhabitable environments, that allude to another everyday life. In this context I am very, very happy, that the Graz University of Technology took the decision in coproduction with our festival to organise this symposium, curated and organized by Roger Riewe with his incredible energy under the title space condition. Spaces, particularly public spaces, are constantly changing faster and faster. What role does architecture play in this context? Can architecture still act or is it doomed to react? The obvious prevalence of the everyday seems to displace the unique, also both are mutually dependent and this is a tremendously important issue, one of the most important current architecture debates, an issue that architecture must face. What would current architecture contribute to society? Globalism versus localism? What synergies can we expect from global issues and local everydayness? Is author–architecture a trail blazer or the combination of architectural conditioning of public space? Is it conceivable, that author-architecture not only includes the determined, but also provides space for the undetermined? What can we, what must we demand? New strategies or even a new radicalism? Welcome to space condition and welcome to steirischer herbst. I wish you a strong and tremendous conditioning of space. Thank you.

ROGER RIEWE

Thank you very much Erich Hödl. Thank you Peter Oswald for the intros. Yesterday, in a discussion we had, preparing this symposium, actually the final discussion after the very many we'd already, but the first one with the moderators on the panels today, we noticed that there is an incredible potential in the space today. People who come here, architects who are here, architectural critics who are here in the audience in a situation which is not really comparable at the moment should make use of the situation today to put forward certain topics, as you expressed already before, in terms of conditioning space, especially public space. But also the moderators we've invited here, would like to focus on very special topics in this sphere of space conditioning, so that's why we reshuffled the whole organisation a little bit, please excuse me for that. Things just tend to happen like this but we think it is a very positive aspect, to have one hour of discussion between the moderators to focus on the topic of the day and then go into the separate groups, having their individual discussions. Also excuse me for having begun a little bit late, but I think this is due to the fantastic opening last night of the steirischer herbst, with an incredible concert from Brenda Fassie – congratulations Peter Oswald for this great show and I hope, we can live up to that, because the steps you set yesterday are quite hard and quite high.

Topic

Roger Riewe with

Bart Lootsma, Neil Leach
in location A

Michael Speaks, Aaron Betsky,
Kari Jormakka, Xavier Costa
in location B

ROGER RIEWE

Ok, now, lets move forward in this discussion. I would like to open the discussion with Michael Speaks. Michael Speaks can you hear me? Ok, Michael!

MICHAEL SPEAKS

So, what, should I actually start straight away?

ROGER RIEWE

Ok, I can hear you. Michael, I would actually open the discussion with you, with you in location B, also to show the audience that this is a video conference, so we can always converse with each other at any time. I think, you've got some very special aspects, especially in bridging space condition with "Latent Utopias", do you mind saying something about that?

MICHAEL SPEAKS

No, but only if you can hear me.

ROGER RIEWE

Yes. Ok cut!

MICHAEL SPEAKS

Well, we had this discussion yesterday afternoon, a number of us...

ROGER RIEWE

Michael, just wait a minute – we can't hear you at the moment. Ok, you can continue.

MICHAEL SPEAKS

I can't repeat that, or I will not repeat that.

ROGER RIEWE

Ok, try again.

MICHAEL SPEAKS

Can you hear me?

ROGER RIEWE

Yes, it's ok.

MICHAEL SPEAKS

Fantastic! I'll scream then. Let me just make a couple of opening statements about the title of the exhibition and maybe the general topic, and I think what we will do is, I don't know what type of order you have in mind after this, especially since I can't see you. It's extremely technologically advanced here, except I am speaking to an audience and I don't see you and you can see me. So I'll just speak and when I am done, you can tell us who the next people are. I am going to read a few things that I jotted down this morning at breakfast. Some of the things I want to say are related to the essay I did on the catalogue, I think almost everybody here has a piece of the catalogue which is really a beautiful and remarkable piece of work and I feel lucky to be part of it. But I want to just make a few initial alterations about the title "Latent Utopias" and the relationship between "Latent Utopias" as a title and as a problem and the issue of experimental architecture. Because for me, they are very different kinds of things. I'd also like to chat from the beginning, that this is about space, I never know really what that means. Especially since for me some of the most interesting people here are product designers or they are at least not people who design space as such. I think that's an initial observation that should be made. So I'm going to, just if you don't mind, read a few comments, that I jotted down at breakfast this morning: Having read several of the catalogue essays including Patrik Schumacher's and Zaha Hadid's title essay "Latent Utopias", but not yet having seen the exhibition, which we will see later on, I wonder if utopia, latent or manifest, is the right way to get at what seems to be occurring today in the most experimental practices of architecture, product design and urbanism. Indeed, as many of the essays in the catalogue suggest, the period, from which we now seem to be emerging that is the period we all collectively called postmodernism – that period was defined against modernist utopian thinking and doing all together. It was, for example, the singular importance of all so called post-modern thinking, to dispense not only with utopian aspirations, but to call into question all depth models, such as the fourteen latent manifest model, from which the title of this exhibition is taken, that distinction, but also the Marxian distinction between base and superstructure, between – the Socratic distinction between signify and signified, but also the political distinction between ideology and science. All those things were called into question by postmodernism and it is out of that, that we seem now to be moving. Now, given all I have seen about the conference and about the exhibition and from the essays that I have looked at – and it is very impressive – it seems to me, that rather than focussing on utopias, we should instead be focusing on experimental practices in architecture and design. Now, whatever else one calls it, that seems to be what the exhibition, in the end, is really about. And I would say, as the professional trendsetters that in architecture and design culture look around for the next big thing, it's the nature of design practices, influenced by new technologies, globalisation and the new commercial realities, that everybody is dealing with in one way or another, that today is pushing the edge of experimentation. To that end I wonder, if we are not emerging into an entirely new intellectual paradigm, that is fundamentally different from the modernist and the post-modernist one, from which we're all fleeing. Modernism was dominated by philosophical truth, by an all knowing vanguard, who having discovered the blueprints of the future, waved them like flags to run from pages of the book of absolute truth in all of our faces. These pages, which we now call manifestos, were the literal guidebooks, that the masses were intended to follow into the future, already seen by the vanguard. In the 1960's and the 1970's these vanguards were fundamentally called into question and this calling into question of modernist vanguards, was leveraged by a then emerging new intellectual paradigm, that many of us later called theory. Now, when I say theory, for me theory is a very, very specialised category of intellectual production. And it's one, I think that's privileged, like unfortunately almost everything today, by the United States. But theory, in my view, was the translation of about eight or ten European philosophers into English and that is specifically into American English and it became a consumer good and then it was sold back to you, as a thing called theory. I, for example, had Dutch students, ask me in the late 1980's, early 1990's, where would the best place in the United States be to study theory and I said, 'My God, why don't you get on a train and go to Paris because that's where all of the theorists are?', and they looked at me as though I were as stupid as I really was and said 'You know, if we go to Paris and study with these people, we study philosophy, but if we go to America and study with these same people and we study these same texts, it's theoretical.' Theory is a sort of fast philosophy, it is consumer's philosophy and it is not connected to the truth. So, I would say in the 60's and 70's, these vanguards, the modernist vanguard practices were called into question, affirmed by this theoretical paradigm, that was emerging. And that theory in many ways enabled all the anti-modernisms that we know about in the 1960's and 70's and 80's, especially post dash modern architecture, as Charles Jencks always wanted us to make sure, that we put the dash in, postmodern classicism, but also deconstructivism, critical regionalism and a whole slew of so called postmodern critical architecture, almost all of these were leveraged by theory and theory itself was enabled by the transformation of philosophy into this consumer good, but also by the transformation of philosophy into a consumer good through linguistics. Everything was in the end about meaning. Now, theory in the vanguards, the vanguard practised and enabled, was resolutely negative. This was its problem. Its principle aim, like the architectures it enabled – decon(-struction), critical regionalism, not to such an extent postmodernism, but even that – its aim was critical. It never offered anything positive. So, for me it's

Michael Speaks

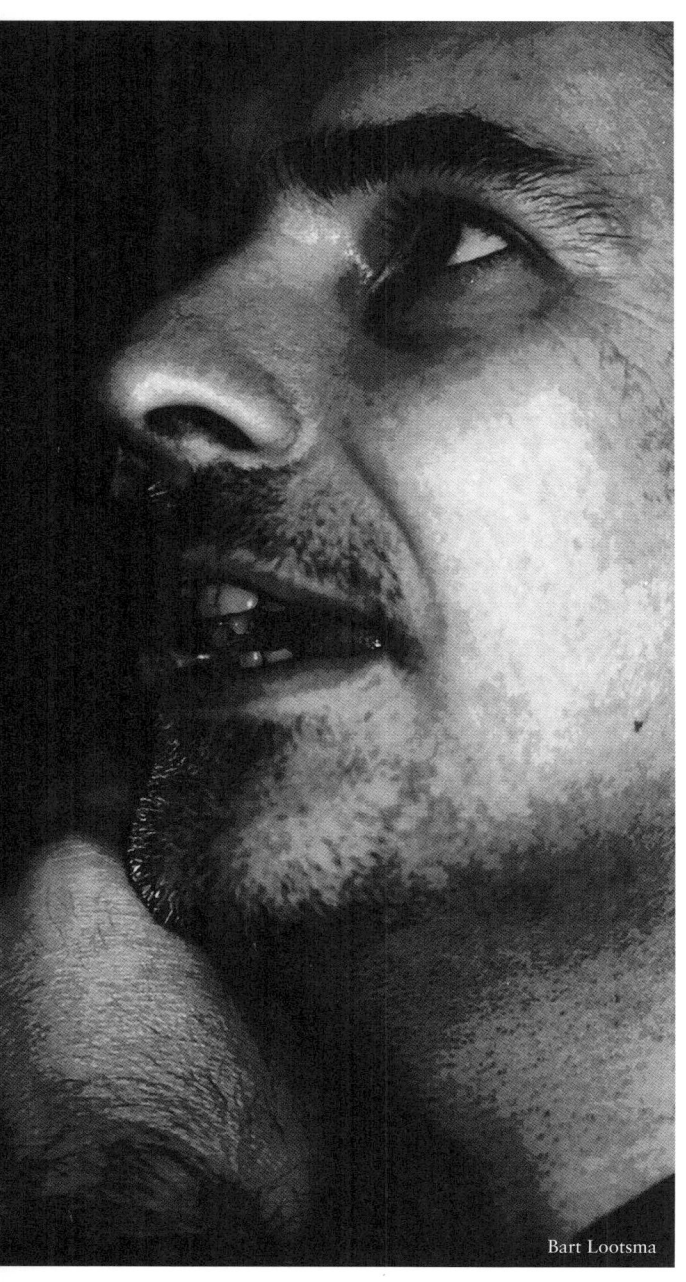

Bart Lootsma

not surprising, that today, after we were moving out of that period, utopia with the pure affirmation, that something else is possible has returned. Now, I think it's an interesting thing, that it has returned as a word, as a concept and as an idea, but for me it's too simple to invoke utopia, latent manifestoes or any other kind of utopia, it's to return in an uncritical way to a modernist project that I think has been completely called into question, and it seems to me, that what we have to do is to rethink precisely what we mean by utopia today. So, if utopia is a return of that, then I for one am completely uninterested. On the other hand, if utopia is a name for the search for something other, for something that's not given in advance, then I think it is well worth considering. Now, in order to make the search for utopia contemporary, it seems to me, that we must acknowledge that a new intellectual paradigm is arising. And for me that intellectual paradigm has already replaced theory. That paradigm I would call intelligence. If theory replaced philosophy in the 1960's and 70's, it seems to me in the 1990's, with the end of the folding episode and with the last waves of obsession, in America and other places with French philosophy, something new, I think, has emerged. And I try to talk about it in greater detail in the catalogue, the piece that I did. But in that piece what I argue for is a new intellectual paradigm that I call design intelligence. Now, design intelligence I would argue, is an intellectual paradigm, that today defines all experimental work. Its approach to knowledge is fundamentally different than the modernist one, which is interested in great ideas. Those great ideas are discovered as truths, written in manifestos and then they are completed in time, they are finalised in time. The modernist vanguards were principally interested in the new and for me the real concern now, is to look at two different versions of the modern and to two different versions of utopia. One of which is historical and one of which is contemporary. It seems to me, if we are to make sense of a contemporary version of utopia, we have to switch our interest – and in fact, I think a lot of the offices, that are involved in this exhibition, are doing this – we have to switch our interest away from an obsession with the new, with discovering the truth and the new and elaborating it in time and switch over to an interest in, what I would call, innovation. There is a real distinction, that the American management theorist Peter Drucker makes between problem solving and innovation. What Drucker says is, that problem solving accepts a problem given and simply completes the problem in a final design. The problem with problem solving is, that nothing is added, no value is added, nothing essentially new is offered nor is anything innovative offered. Innovation, on the other hand, refuses the problem given and, in many ways, tries to redefine the problem and researches not to solve an ultimate to the problem, but really researches in order to reformulate the problem and to produce innovations, that could not have been offered in the form of the problem given, to begin with. So innovation is interested in adding something, it's interested in added value. That, for me I think, is the hallmark of this emerging intellectual paradigm, that I would call design intelligence. Because design intelligences are the techniques, the practices, the dispositions, the approaches to conditions outside architecture, that allow these new offices to add value and, in fact, that allows them to be very different, I think, from the vanguard practices that precede them, either theory driven or philosophically driven. So, maybe that's all I want to say for the moment and maybe that is already too much. But for me there is a real, real... – I have an interest in redefining the context of the debate away from the idea of utopia and looking instead at the idea of experimental practice. And it seems to me, that we really have been through three intellectual models of experimental practice. One, modernism, defined by philosophy and truth, two, theory, and the theory vanguards, which were defined by a critique of modernism and, in fact, were resolutely negative and could offer nothing new and this third paradigm, which for me is absolutely positive and it's about the production of innovative solutions, that return to the practice itself and add to the design intelligence of the practice. So yeah, that for me, for the moment, that's all I'll say, that's probably too much.

ROGER RIEWE

No, I think these three points are extremely interesting in the discussion for today and I hope, we can come back to these points in the further discussion, with the groups, especially you in the groups you will be heading. I would like to take the discussion back to location A, to Bart Lootsma on my right, and it would be especially interesting to know your statements on urbanism and contemporary urban space. How that would fit in this space condition and "Latent Utopias" context?

BART LOOTSMA

Definitely! Good morning. Actually, when I was asked to write a piece for the catalogue of "Latent Utopias", I thought, well, for years I did not want to do that.

MICHAEL SPEAKS

Bart we can't hear you! We allowed that just sort of break in and...

BART LOOTSMA

Is this better?

MICHAEL SPEAKS

Thank you, Bart.

BART LOOTSMA

It's also a bit funny for me. Where was I? Oh yeah! I remember a couple of years ago talking to Herbert Langmaier and Brigitte Felderer and that I said, "well, utopia that's something that people only talk about in Germany", and I could say that as a Dutch guy. That was a very self-satisfied thing. I remember at the time in the 1990's, there was a foundation in the Netherlands that was called 'Utopia is now', actually, which is even more self-satisfied. Winy Maas was a part of that, Roemer van Toorn wrote in that catalogue, some designers from Droog-Design. And there was really this idea, that we had achieved a certain stage in history, that everything was all right. Now, I suppose, everybody knows about the embarrassing kind of events that happened in the Netherlands lately and in a lot of other countries.

MICHAE SPEAKS

Bart, Bart, Bart, I think you have to act like a rock star and try to eat the microphone!

BART LOOTSMA

Should I do that, or shouldn't I? Ok, anyway, as long as you can hear me, ok. Anyway, that was – so suddenly two events came together: on the one hand the kind of strange events in the Netherlands, that kind, where this self satisfaction about a certain level of economy we'd reached in preceding months led to the idea, that it should simply remain like that, on the other hand the question to ask about latent utopias and also here the question for the symposium, if architecture can only react or can it also be a discipline. And indeed, I think, that maybe the thinking in terms about utopia has been a bit lacking in the debate. Of course, the expectations about utopia were always very high and that means, that it was also, let's say, more or less easy, how sophisticated all the books of Lyotard or whoever it may have been, it was also relatively easily, to demonstrate, that utopias would always go wrong. And of course, the idea of a utopia is always immediately interlinked with the idea of a dystopia. Just because there is this formulation of a certain ideal, you can also criticize it and describe the possible negativity to it. Now, when I looked at the catalogue and the exhibition, before I come to Roger's question, because that is something that intrigued me there, when I was looking at it, I was quite struck by the fact, that it is really an architectural exhibition, that goes rather into design than into urban planning. And in a way, one could say, I would not say that, maybe that's the wrong word, we should think about it, but we have talked about architecture for a long time in terms of language, which led to some kind of desperate games with architectural language, the whole series of "isms", that Michael just came up with etc., etc. I have a feeling, that there is something going on in this exhibition. Patrik and Zaha also speak about the relation to art and that brings me to the thing, that there are maybe two or a couple of traditions in utopian thinking in architecture. Should I put it somewhere else? Is this better? Anyway. So there are different traditions. This seems to be better right? There are different traditions. One is a tradition, lets say it starts with the expressionism-people like Bruno Taut, that started from the idea, that there was a new technology, lets say the technology of glass, that enabled architects to produce new shapes and these shapes themselves by working by empathy, by a kind of almost psycho- and physiological reaction of the people, would change society. Although, it was not very clear, how that would happen. But at least, it was a tradition in which, let's say, architects played a crucial role. Now, in this case, that's a very aesthetic tradition and I find this tradition also in the exhibition and in the catalogue here. It would be intriguing to ask particularly Karim Rashid, if Rashid really wants to change the world. If I see it correctly. So, there is somehow this urge in here. On the other hand, the question is, there is a lot of use of existing material in a lot of the projects. That brings me to another thing, because utopia has always been linked immediately to the city. It is about an ideal state, it's about an ideal city and

Aaron Betsky

Xavier Costa

originally about a city state. Now, cities in the world have become very problematic, they have become mega cities or meta cities or whatever, they're all interlinked all over the world, so in that sense, it is very difficult to talk about this kind of island, that Thomas More talked about. But still I have the feeling, that when we speak about, let's say, how architecture can anticipate the development or, when we want to talk about utopias, we should rather talk about urbanism, urban planning, than about architecture. I mean, the effects are very unclear. I would be curious, what kind of effects the architects in this exhibition expect their work to have on people. Do they really expect people to behave differently? But this idea of urbanism is much more important for a real utopia, because then you formulate it in such a way, that it could also be criticized, that it becomes clear and that it can flip from a utopia to a dystopia. Now, there we have seen a long tradition over the last couple of years apart from, lets say, the critical regionalism and all kinds of also urban strategies, that dealt with architectural language and typology. We have seen a whole development into research, in which people like Stephano Boeri, Rem Koolhaas or MVRDV or we ourselves at the Berlage Institute, critically investigated the real processes, that went on in the city. That was a critical process and in the last Documenta catalogue, the last Documenta in Kassel was also almost a kind of documentary festival of all kinds of artists, dealing very critically and registering what was going on in the city. Now you could say, that is a latent utopia, because there is a criticism and because of this criticism of reality you could say, there is something missing. Speaking about urbanism, I think that there might be – when I repeat my catalogue a little bit, there might be two kinds of strategies at this moment in architecture in urbanism. One is still a strategy like the one that MVRDV is using, that tries to solve collective problems with collective solutions. It implies a very strong state, MVRDV very strongly believe in the Western European welfare state and its ability to organize society and the other is almost the opposite, that is, I would say, the way Raoul Bunschoten or also the people like Patrik Schumacher at the AA in London try to deal with it, that is really a kind of bottom up procedure, in which there is a belief, that society cannot be shaped and that there is a much stronger force, that is made up of people working alone, working in kind of ad-hoc collaborations and that that would change society. In both cases I think, that these ideas are very important and it would be important to see how we could implement them in real city planning procedures.

ROGER RIEWE

Thank you Bart. I have not been down at the book stand, yet, but I just hope that the catalogue, everybody is referring to, will be on sale today. That is this catalogue here. It's a fantastic book, fantastic work. Good articles in there and good work inside. I would like to shift the discussion again back to location B to Aaron Betsky. Hi Aaron, I was quite nervous yesterday evening that you hadn't yet arrived and even more nervous this morning when you hadn't shown up and I am actually really delighted to see you beamed on the screens. So, hi and welcome here. Aaron you don't mind focusing a little bit on the topics of 'new spaces' and 'form concepts'?

AARON BETSKY

Now I do wish, I had arrived earlier yesterday. Can you hear me all right? Am I close enough to the microphone? Well, of course my first temptation is to react to what Bart Lootsma said and of course Bart has become so Austrian now, that he does not even understand the absolutely patent, as opposed to latent, irony of the "Utopia Now"-movement and chooses instead to discredit it as just another example of the bankruptcy of the Dutch architecture scene. But that's because he is now in Austrian apple state, but I would also disagree with him that, in fact, what we need to do is extend this kind of research into our experimentation on – if we follow Michael Speaks – a form into the larger scale of urban planning. I think that is exactly what made the utopian tendencies, projects and proposals of modern architecture such giant failures. The tremendous increase in scale, the removal of the standpoint from eye-level to God's eye-level, which proposed giant structures for everyone to inhabit. One of the things that I in fact find very salutary about what I have so far seen about the "Latent Utopias" project is its focus on those things that are smaller than a building, to put it as simply as possible. You look at those objects and images and spaces, interior spaces, that most architects denigrate as being below the level that their intelligence deserves to focus on and therefore are traditionally left for a lesser kind of human being, called an industrial designer or even worse an interior designer, which is usually a woman. At the same time of course, architects have a tremendous way of fetishising exactly those artefacts. I noticed the G4's sitting next to me, and I am sure most architects have one or the other of these latest fetish objects in their possession. Again, that also ties in very nicely with the whole Madonna mania and the horrific way, in which architects, most of them are men, treat women who until recently have not mainly been central in the world of architecture. But, be that as it may, it seems to me, that the very intelligence that is inherent in those objects smaller than building objects, if I can just call them that collectively, in fact, evidences the "Latent Utopias" to which the title exactly refers. Namely a utopia, that is inherent in the objects, images and spaces of everyday life. It's interesting to me, that about eight or nine years ago, General Motors decided that they were going to see if the public was ready to accept a car with a joystick and they did a series of tests and 90 % of the test subjects said, that they would crash their car immediately. Recently both, Ford and I believe it is Nissan, has started developing joystick-cars, because they have found by now, the notion of navigating around, using a mouse or a joystick, is so prevalent, that there are few barriers to its integration into the car and in fact for those of you, who are lucky or unlucky enough, to be so rich, that you have a BMW 7 series, you know, that they have already integrated that into that car for the super elite – obviously the rich get the goodies first and the design intelligence first. That to me signals in fact, that the computer, rather than changing the world and rather than

producing a utopian solution to all problems, as not only architects but also economists promised us a few years ago, has failed, but has been transformed in another way. Let me try to, very quickly, just repeat the argument, that I make in the "Latent Utopias" book. I think if we all do that, then we will save the audience a great deal of money, they can just slip through and look at the pretty pictures and won't have to read the text. The notion was that in fact the digital era, that was upon us, was going to be as much a utopian dawn, as any of the previous technological revolutions have promised. It was going to liberate us all and everyone was going to be able to communicate with everyone, mass customisation meant everyone could have everything they wanted now, wealth and power were going to be absolutely distributed, there would be no more middlemen and any form that you could possibly imagine you could render, draw, model and then build, using everything from a digital pen to a digital cutter. As a result, we would soon live in a completely fluid and flowing network society, where we would all dissolve into a hive-mind and there would be no more human beings and no more world, only continual flow. Not very different from the dream of the crystal palace or any of the other modernist utopias, that have been proposed over the last few centuries. Obviously, this failed completely. None of that. And I repeat, none of that, has come into being. What we are left with, in fact, is this continual image of that promised world, that floates rather prominently in this exhibition as well. Blob forms, fluid forms, forms made with the latest technologies whether they be of representation or using the latest plucky balls, or the latest forms of alloyed steel. Collectively these projects, I would argue, are really in the same class not as architecture, but as science fiction, whether it is written or filmed or on television. Namely it projects, what utopia has already done, from the first time Thomas More came up with the word, it projects another space, not necessarily a good space, but another space, that exists beyond our reality. It does not propose to change the world today, it does not even propose, that we should work towards that world, it rather proposes, that there is the possibility of some other world. Some other world out there. That proposal, in which many architects are today still engaged, can function in one of three ways: it can function first of all as a method of avoidance, it's much more fun to propose a perfect world out there, somewhere, without having to worry about either gravity or clients. It is also a way for the people viewing the utopias, to forget about their lives and believe that in fact they will not just have pie in the sky when they die, but will have a virtual pie right now. As such, it also provides a kind of hope, a hope that in fact such a world might appear, and we might some day, if we live long enough, be able to live in it. A hope also of course, that the architect has, that she or he might be able to make such a perfect place, if they get the perfect client, the perfect software and unlimited budgets. Third thing, that then turns out to be always absolutely impossible is, that utopia functions , as Manfredo Tafuri pointed out quite a long time ago, as a continuous critique of the present – it is always a counter model to what we have today. I would propose to you, that, in fact,

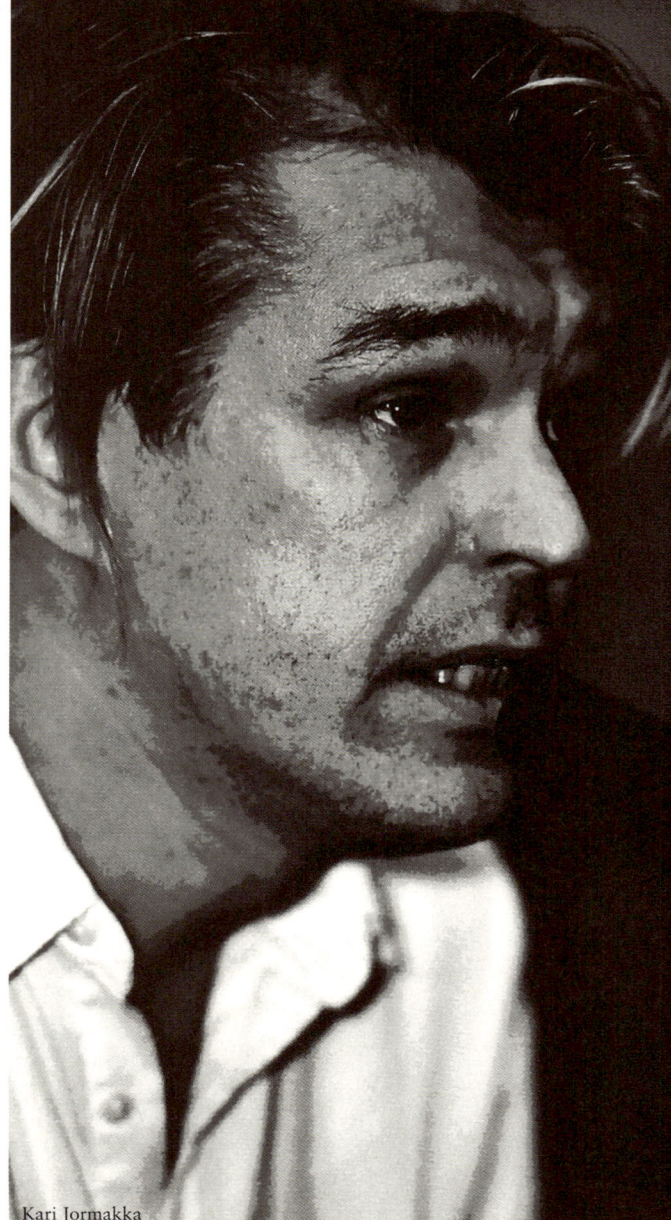

Kari Jormakka

Neil Leach

the blobs, the transact architecture and all the other spectacular forms, that you will see in the exhibition and in the catalogue, are no more than such utopian images. Such projections of avoidance, hope or critique valuable in themselves, but perhaps rather limited. I would propose to you instead that the true latent utopia, the utopia that is, by now, dispersed completely through the object images and spaces of everyday life, functions in a number of different ways. First of all it functions in what UN Studio has called deplanning, as the ability to organize incredibly complicated forces into simple, recognisable, iconic and perhaps even fetishistic shapes, that allow us to understand otherwise completely incomprehensible forces. This is very important, because of course with the dispersal of the tremendous power, that the digital domain offers, comes its complete invisibility and incomprehensibility. I barely grasped, how a computer worked – don't ask me to explain to you how it works. My inability to explain also means that I have a lack of knowledge. If architects can produce models, objects, images that concretely make visible some of these complex flows of information and power, they will have, at least, performed a small part of the utopian task. Second, I think, that the power of computer and communication technologies allow us to make an architecture, that the critic Wouter Vanstipthout has called cheap, dirty and raped. An architecture that has, as Rem Koolhaas said, no money, no details, no need of any fancy thrills. An architecture, that is only as valuable as the amount of money, that is put into it and can easily be changed and broken down. It is a direct challenge to the fetishisation of building, the notion that they should remain as long as possible and the idea, that we should invest as much as possible in buildings, that we should have as big a budget as possible, and proposes instead, that we should try to think of an architecture, that uses computer technology, to make just-in-time-buildings, that can be made out of objects, that are re-used and that can be torn apart and reconfigured as soon as possible. The Berlage Institute, to which Bart already referred, is engaging right now in research as to whether one can think of a city, as something that can be written off in a few years, like a computer, rather than something that needs to stand for a long period of time. Third, of course, one can imagine, that as Greg Lynn is, I think, beginning to propose, though he seems rather resistant to articulate it right now, and I don't think he is here yet, so he can't defend himself, there is the notion, that one can use the most advanced computer-technologies, to make an architecture, that is woven rather than built, that is continuous rather than static and that is fragmentary. In other words, that one can think of architecture not as the making of a solitary object, even a blob, but rather, that one can think of it as a deformation of existing fabric, as posture or addition, as something that only appears when necessary, as a moment of intensification, almost as if all of the computer-technology, that is latent now in most buildings, the wiring, and all the information coursing through these walls, breaks onto the surface and deforms the actual building. That reaches a point of invisibility, that I think points to, what might be the final and most powerful ways, in which new technologies present

the possibility of a latent utopia. And that is, that they not appear at all. That, in fact, we give up the notion, that just because things were designed with computers, for computers or by people using computers, that in fact, we give up the notion, that we need to make images, that are new, different, art, weird and avant-garde as it was said in the introduction today, and rather that we realize, that the computer allows us to make ever more normal, more invisible things. Ford Motor Company, again, experimented and Greg Lynn is very fond of speaking about this, with making a completely computer-steered design in the Ford Taurus and it was rejected by most people. Instead now, the design is inherent. The use of the computer is inherent in the design and the car looks quite normal. The utopian, or shall we say science-fiction side of this, is of course the film Matrix, which is now replacing Blade Runner, as a favourite reference point for architects. In Blade Runner, the zeros and ones are shaping reality, but reality looks absolutely banal and normal. In fact, that is, what is going on. That is reality. Utopia, I would argue, utopia that is latent, would be exactly that, which makes us aware within the seemingly normal images, spaces and objects of everyday life, that they are artificial, that they are unstable, that they are fluid, that they are blobs or trans-architectures, that which would not be immediately evident, patent, but that which would be latent, which would work through irony or, even better, through something, that is so invisible, it cannot even be named, to make us aware of the disturbing uncertainty, disturbing a-human, just not to say anti-human, a-human quality of our reality and propose that we not find solutions to problems, but that we state the problem of our lack of understanding, of what it is in fact, the computers and communication-technologies can do by making us aware of the absurd artificiality of the world we inhabit every day.

ROGER RIEWE

Ok, thank you Aaron, those were quite a few points that you put forward and I'm quite curious to see how this will work in the discussion with Greg Lynn – he will be in your group in the afternoon – so that will be really interesting. After a short discussion yesterday, I would like to put the word forward to Kari Jormakka, who I believe and expect to have still even more aspects in this discussion, which I would like to focus on. Kari please!

KARI JORMAKKA

Ok, I read from my G4 – unfortunately I am waiting for the program that could speak itself, but I just have to read it, yes I haven't seen the exhibition, yet, neither has anyone else, and so I won't really address the work which is presented in there, I think there is a precedent, however, to this situation, I think Oscar Wilde says something like he never reads the books, that he is supposed to review, because that would make him prejudiced, and so in a certain sense I have the freedom now, to talk about things, without having any idea what I am saying. But I'll start with the really great book and the interesting title "Latent Utopias". In a certain sense of course, the combination of latent and utopia seems natural and almost inevitable,

because in a certain sense, so I think as from Thomas More to Michel Foucault, in a certain sense a utopia must always remain latent in reality, because if it's manifested, it can only be manifested in representation, if it becomes real, it is no longer a utopia, hence a utopia is always about emergence and it is always latent in a certain sense. Now, if we ask, what is latent in the project, in the design work, which is included in the exhibition, based on the catalogue, I looked at the catalogue briefly, and it seems, that certain themes reappear in both, the design work and especially in the essays. There are such ideas as to talk about complexity and self-organizing systems, there is a notion of autopoeitic architecture, often generated through the computer for instance. Very often, this discussion is brought into contact with some ideas taken from biology, or from the natural sciences, from physics in some cases and often out of this discussion one gets some sort of conclusion about design-intelligence. Michael Speaks was talking about the re-arrangement of the architectural practice or the design practice in general, the new role of the architect in relation to the economic and commercial forces and so on. Now, in a certain sense it's clear, that the computer holds a great promise here, that's with the use of scientific, often biological or mathematical models involve various kinds of self-organizing systems, one certainly can't avoid or bypass some problems, that arise when we try to apply some schematic utopia models too directly to a much more complicated reality. However, the issue, that I would want to address, is not really this. I would want to talk about the slightly different implication of these self-organizing systems in autopoeitic architecture, that shape itself in response to the new architectural, social and economic reality and these forces, because I think, that a part of this talk is, that there is a kind of a rhetoric, which attempts to give the impression, that this kind of autopoeitic generation of architecture is somehow scientifically justified or even necessary. This is very much a rhetorical figure only, I want to stress that, but it is a rhetoric which is pretty close to what the classic avant-garde was always talking about – I am thinking of this famous statement by Mies in the Twenties when he said, that we have to accept the new economic and social realities as a fact, they take their course, dictated by destiny and blind to values. Or, if you think of Le Corbusier, when – la ville radieuse – he is talking about architecture, which is also necessary in a certain way, even though perhaps more autonomous, when he is talking about how the plan is, what is right, the plan postulates or posits indubitable realities, realities that you cannot even doubt. Now, this kind of rhetoric is interesting to me, and I seem to see some of this stuff in the work and in the essays. And in a certain sense it makes sense, because, of course, any architects that aspire to being actually built, must somehow respond to economic realities and things like that. But there is of course also a big difference when we think about "Miesean" realism and the new realism. One of the things that we got from the post-modern generation was the idea, was the conviction, that the world is a lot more complex and plural than the modernists have suspected. And this of course means, that instead of trying to find fixed ideals, any clear set-up values, one has to find ways of managing complexity and perceiving complexity in a situation where very few shared values can be appreciated. Now, the situation that we have today – perhaps the major difference between the modernist generation and our generation is, that no master-narratives can be found except for one, which is of course the master-narrative of the end of history. Now, in the session – I want to make this very brief – so in the session to follow, which I think is coming pretty soon after this one, I want to ask some questions and as the people participating in that session define their positions relative to some issues, such as 'how does one indeed deal with this... – what are the political or ethical implications of these new design possibilities, what kind of issues, what kind of an ethic could we derive from this autopoeitic architecture, whether it is computer-generated or otherwise generated? Are there any limits to the design-intelligence and who might set the limits? Is there anything like the natural selection that operates in the world of nature, that in the world of architecture or design could identify these more successful facts of experimentation? I think, that I will leave it at that, thank you.

Continued on page 49

Interviews 1

Our work is focused on the attempt to develop a new language of architecture that is able to organise and articulate an increased level of social complexity. This includes the attempt to organise and express dynamic processes within a spatial and tectonic construct. This ambition operates on many scales: from the organisation of whole urban quarters, via various building scales, down to the interior furnishings. The challenge is to increase architecture's capacity to spatialize and articulate the complexities of contemporary life processes with its multiple interpenetrating agendas.

Our diverse cultural backgrounds really fade into the background as we cope with the challenge to creatively interpret the next stage of our internationalized post-industrial civilisation. We are true cosmopolitans who would like to refrain from speculating about the influence of local national experiences. Any such speculation can only serve to distract from the issues of the current metropolitan condition.

The global culture of contemporary avant-garde architecture does not dismiss the need for a careful contextual embedding of any architectural intervention. Quite to the contrary: A highly contextual approach is one of the a prioris of contemporary architectural culture. This is what qualifies contemporary avant-garde architecture over the modernist and post-modernist precursors. While modernism was context-blind, post-modernism was rigidly context-bound on the basis of a selective and reductive reading of "context" in terms of a privileged, dominant typology. Our type of contextualism is about the establishment of a rich network of connections and affiliations within a complex contextual field.

Computer technology, i.e. the new digital design tools, have had an important and increasing influence on our work over the last 10 years. This concerns primarily the handling of increasingly complex geometries within our designs. However, the desire for such tools to be imported from the animation industry originated in the fact that the tendency towards complexity and fluidity was already manifest in the work before those tools were available. Our elaborate techniques of projective distortion – deployed as a cohering device to gather a multitude of elements into one geometric force-field – were setting the precedence of contemporary computer based techniques of deformation.

We have been teaching for most of our careers as architects – ever since we graduated. The student body is a great resource of exploration. Here new techniques, themes and ideas can be pursued with an uncompromised focus. This is a welcome pendent to the world of commissions where all sorts of particular pragmatic constraints channel the designers effort. The tension between principled experiments on the one hand and quite particular reality checks on the other hand creates a fruitful dialectic. New ideas are always measured against real constrains and real tasks are always confronted with new ideas.

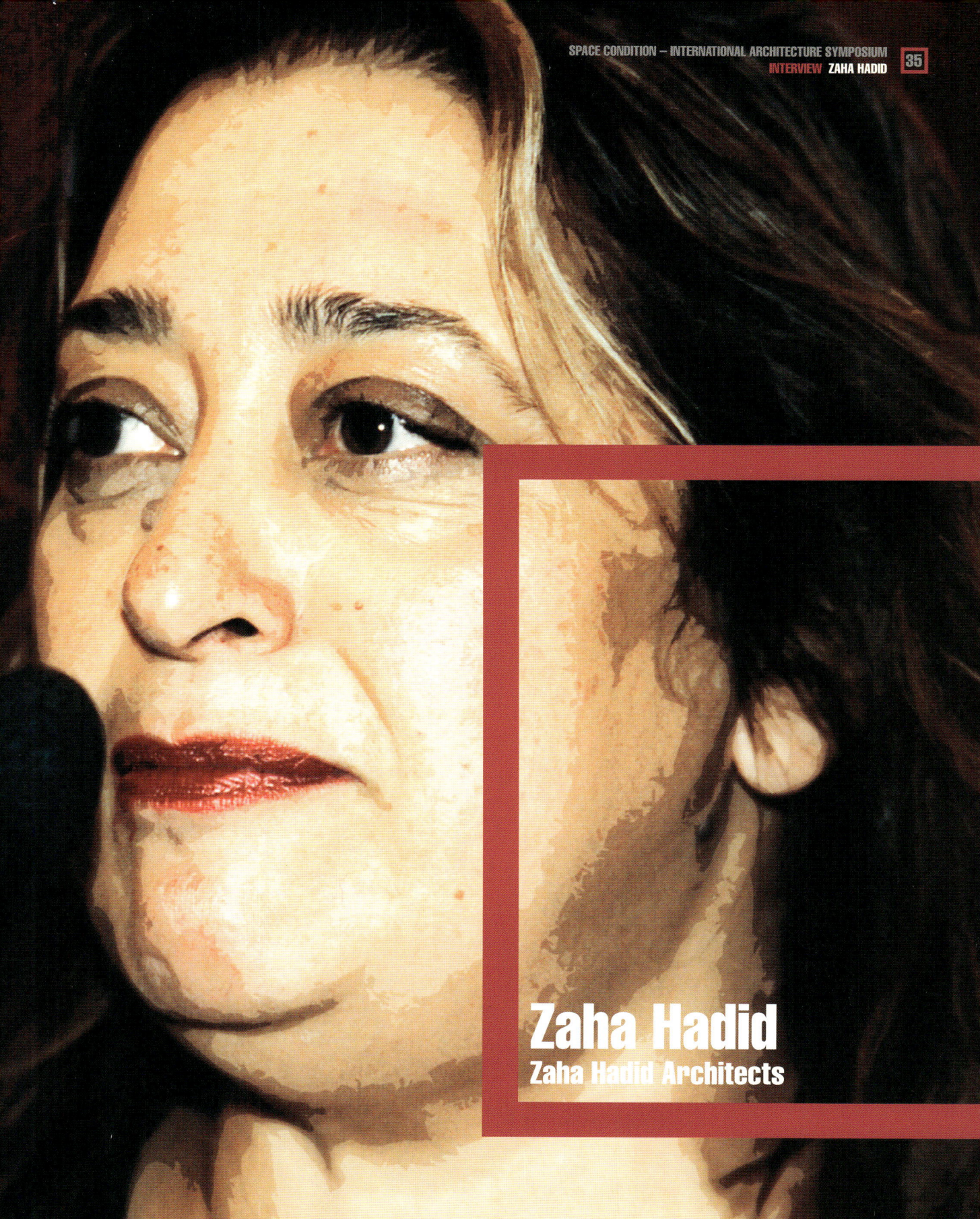

Zaha Hadid
Zaha Hadid Architects

Hani Rashid
Asymptote

Elisabeth Nöst-Kahlen

My first question is, how would you characterize your work and your architecture and what's the typical point in your architecture?

Hani Rashid

Well, we always call our office a research-studio. The architecture of the studio has always essentially revolved around experimentation, research and the implementation of this research into the real world. The general basis of everything is spatiality, so we have taken on a position that anything that comes in to our world has a spatial dimension and would be something to tackle as a practice. Even things as simple as a web-environment, a virtual reality-environment, a building, an interior or an urban plan, an object or furniture – they all imply spatial issues and we are researching what kind of new territories can be discovered within the primaries of those projects and problems.

The basis of the research is a sort of marriage of technological possibilities and innovation with the human dimension – things that are sometimes hard to measure like desire, metaphysics or even the poetic. We are not against those kinds of intrusions into the technological field, in fact we think, that they are making architecture vivid and human.

Elisabeth Nöst-Kahlen

So, how does your cultural background influence your work?

Hani Rashid

Well, my cultural background is diverse and strange, but very modern, I guess. My father is Egyptian, my mother is British. First I was brought up in Europe, then in Canada. I went to school in the United States, now I live and work in New York. But New York isn't really the United States, it is a kind of hyperrealization of the contemporary world.

I think in many ways, the modern nomadic condition of being from many places and assimilating those into a state of being is a status that we all have, whether we are from a small town in Austria or a large city in Europe or America, because the "post-Marshall Mc Luhan-global village" has become a global megapolis.

We are all implemented in a kind of interesting nomadic situation. We may come from a particular place, but we deal with each other with the internet, we travel very easily, we are able to break down boundaries and borders and languages rapidly and so that situation is a very, very contemporary situation and my own cultural situation is in the line with a situation that is more and more normal as we go into the future.

Elisabeth Nöst-Kahlen

So, it doesn't influence you a lot?

Hani Rashid

No, the particular place has a remarkable influence when you acknowledge that you are also part of the world, be that through technology, be that through your philosophical position in the world. If you see yourself as locally tied to a global situation or globally localized, then I think you are engaging the reality of our world. We are globally localized human beings.

Elisabeth Nöst-Kahlen

So, what exactly does place mean to your architecture?

Hani Rashid

Our very first projects were all very large-scale projects and they were in different places. The first winning competition was in Los Angeles, our second big competition was in Alexandria/ Egypt, we also did a project in Tokyo. Now we work in places all over the world and the most important thing is to figure out how to assimilate and bring together the local conditions at some abstract level of understanding.

I do believe that cities have a DNA like human beings, I do believe that there are mappable differences between one place and the next but, like DNA, it's an abstract mathematical and scientific procedure to find out what these differences are.

It is not a matter of saying in Vienna, for example, there is a certain kind of historic tradition in ornaments and therefore I should put ornaments into my building – that's absurd – but you could say that in Vienna there are certain tendencies in art and culture, in music and history, there are things located that can be brought into a contemporary architectural discourse.

Elisabeth Nöst-Kahlen

You use digital tools – how does this influence your work and your design?

Hani Rashid

The computer and the digital tools that we have at our disposal are changing everything.

They are having an incredible impact in every kind of science and also in architecture. It also influences our design because any technique that has been deployed has influenced the designs we came up with. I would argue that Louis Kahn, for example, was very influenced by the materials he made models and studies with. Also Saarinen, let's say, was able to employ other kinds of forms and structures by virtue of his technologies and tools. We now have digital tools that let us see things that we were never able to see physically before.

They allow us different ways to see what we are producing or thinking about and the thing I used to do with my students at Columbia University was to have them use the computers as a research studio and to have real experience in digital that they could bring up to reality then.

Heywon Seo

My first question is, could you explain the meaning and the pronunciation of the name "dECOi"?

Mark Goulthorpe

Well, the first time we used it, it was a code for an international competition and it's pronunciation fascinated the jury and the organizers of the competition so it worked very well for us. And you can pronounce it as you like.

Heywon Seo

Ok, how would you characterize your architectural work?

Mark Goulthorpe
dECOi

Mark Goulthorpe
Architecture?

Heywon Seo
Architecture.

Mark Goulthorpe
Perhaps because I've been living in a foreign country, I am not subject to the normal professional protocols that one might expect if I was living in London.

I think that has forced a sort of slightly over-academic approach to practice. So dECOi is a research-based practice – which is unusual – in the way, that we are spending almost too much time thinking about things because we have been disenfranchised from the ordinary opportunity of architects.

So I often feel I am a boxed intellect, living in the wrong place. But I think it has been both: a disadvantage and an advantage, to be in a kind of position of disenfranchisement because it does allow you to speculate and to think through how one might practise differently in the absence of practising. Now it has been ten years of speculation and I hope, that will materialize into a new form of practice.

Certainly, being so estranged has meant that I sorted out linkages to various different people and organisations. And so dECOi is a loose network and we are using the computer principally as a communication device. We are linking to programmers in Austria,

to mathematicians in England and so on and that offers a very different model of practice than the traditional "everything-under-one-roof" because we are a network of technical specialists.

Heywon Seo
You have worked with some of the world's most renown architects like Richard Meier and Norman Foster. How did they influence your architecture? Have they?

Mark Goulthorpe
Oh, for sure. I think, if you work in a place like Meier's or Foster's, you can't help but be influenced enormously. I do, though, think, that my experience, particularly at Richard Meier's office, left me puzzling about the single-signature and I think, when I set up dECOi, it was certainly a critique of the single-signature-office, even if that wasn't clearly articulated in my head at that time. dECOi has allowed groups of people to come together and operate within it without the feeling that there is just a single person who is the most important. From the inception dECOi was inherently sensing that there were other modes of practice and as digital technology is coming we are actually realizing, that the very nature of architectural practice will go through a profound restructuring. It demands a very different attitude to signature and authorship.

Foster still fascinates me. He is someone who has quite clearly tackled the very principles of construction and construction industry. He spent his formative period looking at prefabricated systems in America and then he took that back to Europe, offering a really radical critique of what is actually concrete industry.

I can't help thinking that much of the eco-architectural work that is going on at the moment is the same kind of approach that Foster had. People are looking at the next technology, which is digital and digital manufacturing techniques and I am trying to speculate what will be the outcome of the efficient modes of practice.

Foster is still large in my mind, even if the model of the office and the work that is being produced now isn't necessarily what I am interested in, but I think it is his mode of practice that is compelling and that can teach us a lot.

Heywon Seo

How many people are in your team and how is your team organized?

Mark Goulthorpe

Typically there are three or four people operating as a traditional architectural hub and then we are outreaching to probably four or five others, mathematicians, programmers and parametric modellers and in particular making

links to universities like UCO and RMIT, the principle ones, where research is happening within universities to bridge the practice. I think that the role of the universities is incredibly important because the universities have time and possibilities to research, which small practices simply can't.

Heywon Seo

You have had some projects in Asia. What was the great difference to planning in Europe?

Mark Goulthorpe

Well, the remarkable thing in Asia is, you are operating in a context of enthusiasm and open-mindedness. There is no nostalgia, there are too few architects and there is an enormous desire to construct rapidly. I was astonished by the opportunities that exist for young architects and the willingness of people entertain speculative ideas. In Europe, where I am operating now, it is a very different pitch. It is extremely nostalgic, laboured and politicised. There is a very different spirit of "can do" in Malaysia – and everything is "can do", even if they can't. There is a fantastic optimism, which I find very refreshing and therefore I miss Asia.

Heywon Seo

Is there something you want to say to the students of today?

Mark Goulthorpe

One thing is, that I think we are in a period of technical and technological assimilation. We are looking at these new tools which reconfigure practise as we know it in a broad sense. There is a tendency to try to shorten the duration of architectural education. Students don't want to be taught extensively, they want to do it on their own, which is a mistake. I think, architecture is a long and deep discourse and whether you are working with a digital tool or not, good preparation is absolutely vital to understanding the complexity of the thing.

The second thing is to look at the digital tools attentive. There are three ways you can use the computer: you can work algorithmically, programmatically or parametrically. And everybody should be coming out of a school of architecture with a knowledge of all three approaches and a specialisation in at least one. So, you should be assimilating an algorithmic, a programmatic or a parametrical potential and I don't see many schools of architecture that are taking these tools seriously enough. I think, students would be advised to treat these tools with a good deal more gravity than is encouraged at the moment.

Eva Grubbauer
Welcome, Marie Therese Harnoncourt and Ernst Fuchs. Which project would you take as an introduction to your work, and how would you characterise your work?

Marie Therese Harnoncourt
We are mainly interested in the production of spaces that have a certain kind of intensity. We create this intensity, this charging up of a space, through the design process and we also believe that by means of such spaces one can achieve new programmatic definitions. In the general building debate at the moment there is hardly any concept of space. Only useable floor space, square metres and costs, whereas we believe that

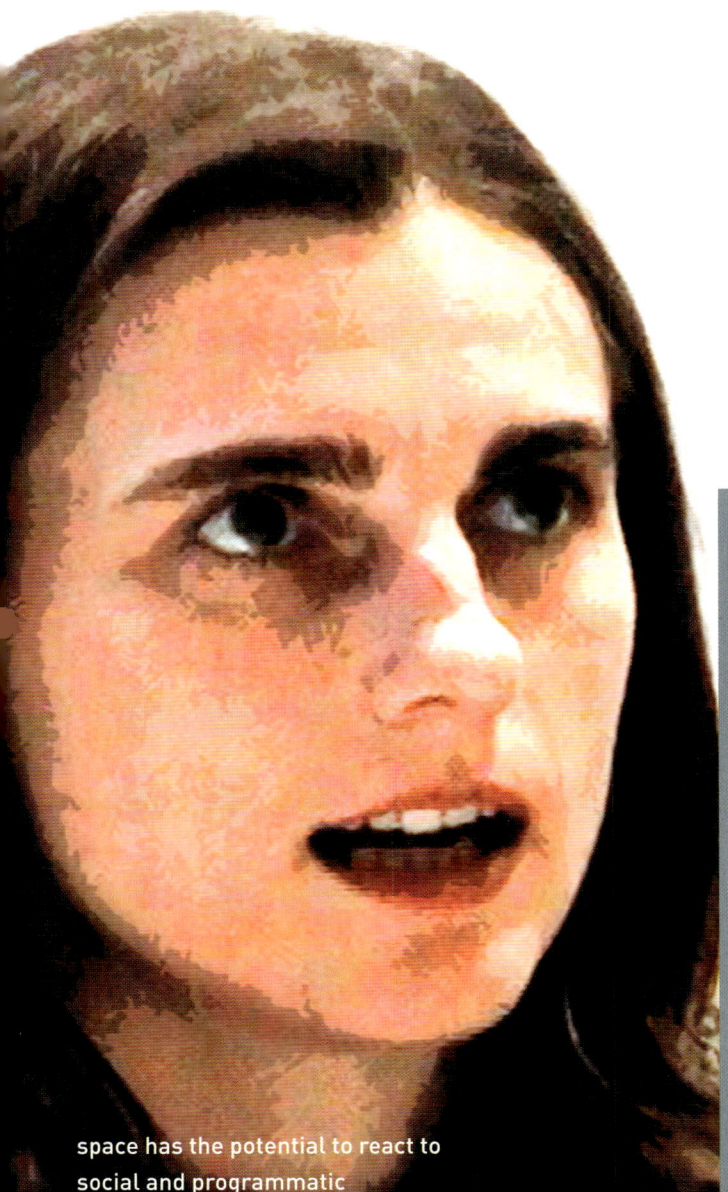

space has the potential to react to social and programmatic conditions and this is why we focus on finding such unpredictable spaces.

Eva Grubbauer
To what extent does the context of the place play a role – you are not only talking about interior spaces?

Marie Therese Harnoncourt, Ernst J. Fuchs
The next ENTERprise

Marie Therese Harnoncourt

No, I am talking about buildings, installations and urbanism. At the beginning of a project is the collection of information, both factual and associative: this is why the environment is always important. The way one then connects and interweaves things and arrives both at form and programme may then vary. What is essential, however, is that we do not enter the design process with a fixed image in our minds. We want to discover new angles by triggering questions in the process. This is why within this context we usually talk about finding space, and not inventing space.

Eva Grubbauer

To what extent does your own cultural background and your education have an influence on your work?

Ernst J. Fuchs

That is an essential aspect. Personal background, education, the place where you grew up: these influence the development of your interests, your viewpoints and your perception of the environment.

Eva Grubbauer

In reference to a project, can you point to a concrete example of this?

Ernst J. Fuchs

We are generally very interested in process-oriented work, which also means that things from outside are drawn in, that there are discussions with other teams, triggering communication on a certain topic.

Hence, personal surrounding and encounters are important, the pleasure of developing ideas and the emotional relationship one develops with the project. Even if this is not immediately visible or useful to the observer, we are convinced that the spaces conceived by us convey our personal emotions.

Eva Grubbauer

Do you accompany a project in the implementation process?

Ernst J. Fuchs

We started with smaller projects and in our first one we were the clients. This means we developed both programme and concept and then realised the space. It is, however, also about the scale and, from a certain size on, it's no longer easy to decide

whether to carry out a detailed planning or not, instead one must fight for it. Basically, I think that the first thoughts one formulates reappear in the way a detail is conceived. This cannot be separated; only the degree of abstraction differs. On the level of project development and formulation, one must work with methods of making things visible for implementation. Using the tools that feel closest to us. Whether this is a drawing or a model or a representation on the computer varies in our work.

Eva Grubbauer

What do you think about theoretical discussion, about events like this one, and to what extent do they influence your work?

Ernst J. Fuchs

Theory is important for us in that it is one of our concerns to work on a language-related, conceptual level and to find and create new concepts. This is why we almost always find ourselves in a theoretical discussion and think this is a very interesting symposium. Of course one would like to communicate one's own projects on a theoretical level also and include the experiences in new projects. We have also realised some works on a very abstract level, in which we tried to find out whether it was possible to avoid frozen concepts and find new designations.

Marie Therese Harnoncourt

I would like to add something from a completely different standpoint: I think that, particularly in an international symposium, it is interesting to see that one can feel the training of the others in different places. Also the way in which people embark on their practical work differs considerably. Our beginnings were certainly not particularly academically influenced. We started from our own basis with thinking out things and these would be implemented partially on a 1:1 scale. For instance, starting to reflect in the city on the city. Approaching ideas you have in your mind but cannot put your finger on, by means of activities. In America at the outset there is a much more theoretical discussion; we prefer the emotional approach. Opening up and having a look around in order to develop things further, thereby finding our own position. One constantly finds oneself in a development process and we have reached a time in which fields of argumentation are opening up, coming from different areas to ideas that we have partially implemented, but without large concepts or aims. Now we are reflecting on these ideas again and placing them within an environment.

Ernst J. Fuchs

I am convinced it is essential that during one's studies one starts to develop conceptual thinking. Without a strong concept and the ability to verbalise this concept, it is barely possible to implement the building structures one has in mind. We need the theoretical background upon which we can place the ideas we are focussing on.

Marie Therese Harnoncourt

But conceptual thinking cannot be equated with the academic approach.

Ernst J. Fuchs

No. I never use the term "academic", as it's not one that springs to mind for me.

Eva Grubbauer

Does this mean that we have to differentiate between academic and conceptual thinking and practical work?

Marie Therese Harnoncourt

Conceptual thinking is that which is abstract.

Ernst J. Fuchs

This is why it is not easy to answer the question about concrete project examples; ultimately each project, small or large, has its own meaning and importance within the overall context.

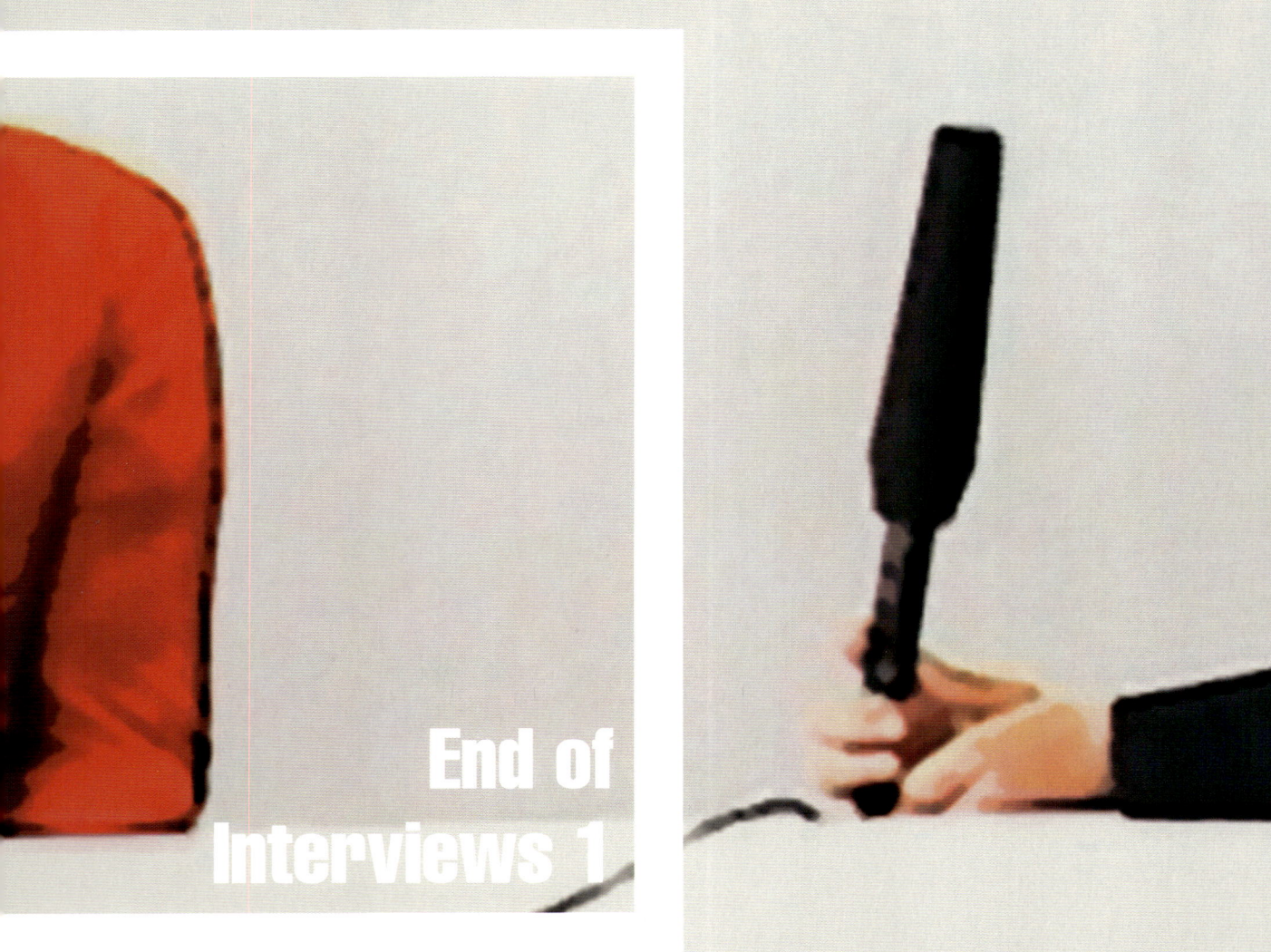

End of
Interviews 1

Topic continued from page 32

ROGER RIEWE

Ok, thank you very much, Kari Jormakka. Neil Leach, I assume you have very specific aspects to add to this discussion.

NEIL LEACH

Yes, I think this is actually turning into a really interesting dialogue between two different rooms and I would just like to respond, just briefly first of all and in particular actually to Michael Speaks' comments. I respect Michael a lot, but I would just like to challenge him on a couple of questions. Firstly, on the issue of utopia. Maybe this is a difference of Europe and America. In Europe the notion of utopian thinking is still alive and well, I think this is very important. utopia to my mind speaks of kind of two issues: one of the possibility of using the imagination in order to imagine a better world, but also primarily a kind of a social dimension, that should be a better sort of social world. It seems to me that there is a kind of writing to this project which is the political and social issue. And I think, that should be kept alive as one of the inherences of the modern movements, of modernity, we must not relinquish a criticality about it. Secondly, I was very much interested in Michael's anti-theory theory, as a theorist myself, I suppose I should possibly defend theory in some senses. It seems to me, there are two types of theory broadly: One is a theory, that is kind of based on prescribed rules, the sort of theory, that we inherited from Vitruvius, for example. There is also another kind of reflexive sort of theory, one, which is not set in any way, but is constantly mutating, adapting, that is a process of critical reflexivity, which is something I think we have to sort of hold on to and that is what I would call theory and it still – it should be very much alive and well. Just briefly in regard to my own particular topic which is on the term 'digital tectonics', so I should perhaps just explain that particular term. When I was teaching at Columbia in the 1990ies, someone said to me: "Really, the work that you've been doing so far on philosophy and theories is all very well, but the debate has shifted on, it's all about technology now, it's about computation and methodology, about new materials and so on." And I guess, my kind of work has responded to that, in particular to the context of what was happening at Columbia at that time. At that moment, there was a divide between those people who were producing astonishingly a sort of fertile, rich and seductive imagery, using MAYA programming and other computer-techniques and on the other side, people like Kenneth Frampton, who was saying, that actually architecture is not about the potential of computer-programs, but about the tectonic capacities and materials. And to some extent, you know, I think that Kenneth Frampton was absolutely right there. But nevertheless there comes a time, when that sort of, those two worlds begin to sort of collapse, when the computer is no longer used for sort of science fiction, but actually as part of the tectonic fabrication of architecture itself.

And I think, what would be interesting now is a kind of new paradigm, a new shift, where people are using these new techniques, these new processes, linked to the computer, in order to fabricate a new material world. It's not about science fiction, it's actually about a kind of concrete reality. And in a sense, that is the sort of topic that I would like to address in my particular session, but above all, I want to sort of keep alive this question about critical reflexivity, but there should be a kind of criticality to it, that has a sort of social dimension. And that doesn't necessarily mean, a kind of a theory in the abstract sense, it could be a kind of material thinking. But above all, it is a kind of a process, revaluating and imagining a better future world.

ROGER RIEWE

Thank you very much, Neil. Last but not least Xavier Costa in location B. I would like to hear a few aspects of your topics that you've put forward on aesthetics and culture architecture. What are yours?

XAVIER COSTA

Yes, I hope that the microphone is working well and you can hear me. Well, it seems inevitable, that we are all addressing the very title of this exhibition and publication, that, of course, is our reference today. The choice of the term utopia is such a provocative selection, that inevitably compels us to discuss it. Of course, the term utopia has become one of the greatest taboos in recent years for the architectural discourse and the architectural debate. In a way,

the term utopia was one of the few terms, that managed to summarize, to provide the synthesis of the objectives of modernism, that had been very thoroughly discussed and of course criticized. If we look at a text like Peter Burger's "Theory of the Avant-garde" which is I think among others a good summary of how the very notion of utopia is providing his capsulation of modernist thinking. So, utopia has been presented during the past years as an objective of modern design, that brings these issues of elitism, of authoritarian understanding of design, that has again been criticized thoroughly. Now, how come we are interested in rescuing this term, in reintroducing it in our discussion? As it was discussed in the previous discussions, the return of utopia seems to renegotiate some aspects of modernism that we believe are still active, are still with us, and one of them would be the possibility of experimentation or a radical research, a base work, that in the wake of pragmatism, that has been emerging these past years, seems to be a necessity to reintroduce and to reconsider these possibilities. I think, an important point that is made in the catalogue, that also helps to clarify this question of utopia today, is Patrik Schumacher's introduction. He makes two points, he refers to the end of the grand narratives as one of the elements, that makes utopia, let's say part of the past, and not part of the present, and the other one is the autonomy and self-reference of architectural discourse and architectural practice, that has been also present with us and that would exclude the possibility of utopia. Well, I said these two parameters could be useful for us as the basis for this discussion. The self-referential closure of architectural practice is an issue, that has been reappearing and that is still with us nowadays; is architecture tending to create a space of its own, where it can play with freedom in this form based research, or is architecture more in favour of opening an effective and direct dialogue with the other forces in society and in culture? This relationship between architecture and culture, that Roger was asking about, I think would be a good ground to carry this discussion to. To refer to the first presentation by Michael Speaks: I feel, when Michael – also in a provocative way – equates architectural design with product design, is opening a series of very relevant questions. In product design we accept that the forces of economy, the forces of the market, the forces of present culture and also of mass culture, whether we like them or not, are inseparable from the design-process. Of course it's not easy for us to accept that architectural design could be equated with product design, because then we would have to accept, that this series of forces would be acting similarly in our design-process. In a way to accept the product design is also to definitely leave aside any possibility of utopian ground for architecture. I think therefore that – and again in relation to the recent discussion on pragmatism, that has been emerging in these past months, probably more in the American context than in the European context, to bring utopia back on the table, is definitely a provocation, but it can be useful as a starting point for us. I hope that in the sessions today, we get to say something about it. Thanks.

ROGER RIEWE

Ok, thank you very much Xavier Costa. I think, everybody has noticed, there is an incredible amount of points being put forward here, which will be a rich potential for opening up a debate and everybody is now, of course, waiting for the architects to show up and see, what they have to say in the confrontation with these points.

After a short break we will see in location A, which is here: MVRDV, ocean D, Patrik Schumacher, the next ENTERprise, chaired by Kari Jormakka and in location B: Asymptote, Ocean North, Pichler-Traupmann, Softroom, being chaired by Bart Lootsma.

Space Condition Part 1

Kari Jormakka with
Patrik Schumacher (Zaha Hadid Architects),
Greg Lynn (Greg Lynn FORM),
Tom Verebes (ocean D), **Marie Therese
Harnoncourt** (the next ENTERprise)
in location A

Bart Lootsma with
Hani Rashid (Asymptote), **Kivi Sotamaa**
and **Michael Hensel** (ocean NORTH),
Christoph Pichler and **Hannes
Traupmann** (Pichler & Traupmann),
Oliver Salway (Softroom)
in location B

BART LOOTSMA

I hear that we can start. They are still having coffee. Kari, do you hear me? Moonstation calling for Kari Jormakka?

KARI JORMAKKA

Houston, we have a problem!

BART LOOTSMA

Kari, are you ready to start? Can you hear us?

KARI JORMAKKA

Cool, I was supposed to start first. Let me start this session first by introducing the people, but before introducing them, I would simply say, that what I would like to do is to ask some questions concerning values and ethics and politics, because I think, that every utopia in a certain sense holds a political promise or at least a promise of a political critique, and those would be political and ethical and such issues. And I will – by way of addressing the problem, I will first simply name the members of the panel. Probably an introduction is not really needed – but I will do it anyway. On my extreme right is Tom Verebes from ocean D. ocean D, as you might know, is this off-shoot of the ocean network, that was originally created in the AA, and which has sponsored, I think, now three different offices, more or less, and it is a network, where, in all of the three cases I think, several basic issues are raised, concerning, for instance, the nature of design. I think, the ocean network from the beginning on has been experimenting with different levels of design, different kinds of design, different possibilities of production and so on. ocean D in

particular, which is a firm based in Boston, New York and London, also wants to straggle between different levels of design and also these new situations, where one might really individualize the design to the particular needs, instead of having the basic modernist mode of production. Now, some of those issues, I think, will come up, concerning the role of the architect, the role of the designer and the possibilities of both, the design and the production process, to redefine a new role. Then to my right is Mr. Greg Lynn, whom I think I would not need to introduce, I think that everybody here knows Greg's work and I am very excited to see, how he will respond to these particular issues. So I will simply move on to the next person on my left, Marie Therese Harnoncourt, who is here representing the next ENTERprise, a company which she shares with Ernst J. Fuchs. Unlike many other young architects, who are working on experimentation, the next ENTERprise, and the previous office called the poorboysENTERprise have actually been able to realize some of their projects and so they have that unique perspective of knowing what it means to try to translate a utopia or an experimentation into something real. And then finally, we have Patrik Schumacher, whom you also know from his work with Zaha Hadid and his own work as a designer, a theorist and a philosopher. He is also, of course, the co-curator of the show that we will be able to see tonight. So I would like to begin in fact with Patrik. In the catalogue he has written an essay, a very interesting essay, where many of the themes that I would like to address today, are also discussed, in particular the idea of this autopoiesis in architecture. And he uses this idea of these self-organizing systems, this idea of these self-generating intelligent order also to define the role of architecture, so that architecture has something of the autonomy of a discipline, and yet is not unresponsive to various forces, – social, economic, political forces. So I would like to begin by asking Patrik, how he would design..., how he would derive from this notion of autopoeitic architecture a kind of a ethical or political basis. Is architecture a discipline? Does it have limits? Does it have a kind of disciplinary basis or a discourse, which would allow us somehow to form an ethics for design?

PATRIK SCHUMACHER

I think I'll take the opportunity to make a few comments also with respect to the series of introductory notes which we listened to this morning and I think which raised the stakes for a very high level of reflection and I am grateful for a series of quite serious questions both with respect to the concept of "Latent Utopias" and also challenges to the work and what it means. And of course we are fully aware that the notion of utopia has been disintegrated and it is a kind of tricky one to introduce, that is precisely one reason why we brought it back in. I think Neil Leach brought forward the notion that, you know... – it might be difficult to just kind of forget about it and when I was invited by the director of the festival steirischer herbst, Peter Oswald, he was just simply inviting me to show current architectural utopias. And my immediate response was: "Hang on, this is a bit naive, these kinds of... – don't exist in the world today." At the same time it was clear, that if there is

a discipline of architecture, which distinguishes itself from just mere pragmatic building and the reproduction of clients demands, there must be criteria, which guide a kind of disciplinary discourse. And so something has to replace this notion of progress, which has been questioned as well, and I think of course there have been notions about history, the end of the "great narrative" etc., but at the same time it is obvious that history has not come to a stand-still. The problem around there is, that we can no longer anticipate its shape. And therefore we are moving from, I mean... – Michael Speaks offered the notion of experimental practices, as replacing this kind of very long tradition of architecture being involved in imagining the good city, the good life and everybody understood that this is a requirement to give sense and meaning to design speculation and what is supposed to replace this, and it does to a certain extent, is experimental practices, but this backs the questions about the criteria. What I think replaces this notion of rationalistic blueprint projecting a better life is, in a way, the paradigm of the evolution brought forward into the historical process. And so I prefer to talk about mutations on a number of existing conditions, recombinations and on what is offered up for a kind of selection process, which involves... – which the architect can no longer take upon himself. Maybe to a certain extent yes, you start to select your own proliferation elements and filter down and then there is a selection process, a process of appropriation and also experimentation on the part of the users and clients and then, from that, you move into reproduction. So, mutation, selection, reproduction are the kind of stages, which represent evolution and it's very important, that these stages, and mechanisms, evolutionary mechanisms of mutation versus selection, versus reproduction are in a deeply differentiated and complex social process. And in my essay, which Kari is referring to, I used the amazing kind of theoretical enterprise of Niklas Luhmann, who theorized contemporary conditions under the notion of autopoiesis and one of the reasons, we've moved away from this notion of a blueprint-utopian condition, why theorists sooner or later have to come forward to talk about the end of the grand narrative and the bankruptcy of these straight forward blueprints is the fact that society – first of all it is no longer easily identified, where is it located, is it global world civilization, is it particular societies, which could be addressed like the European welfare state, of course there is a lot of criticism, that this is kind of on-the-way-out and there is nobody guiding the process. So there is no address anymore, to which you could kind of talk about what we should do or what they should do, what society should do. It does not have a single address, it does not have a control centre, it does not have a single self-description any more. What we are looking at instead is a series of differentiated, self-organized and self-propelling sub-systems of social communication and I argue, that architecture is one of them. I mean obviously Luhmann distinguishes the economy as a quite separate, autonomous domain, quite independent, no longer under control of the political system. Then there is the science with the international discourse, which is certainly no longer under control of the political regime, of any political

regime. There is the art, the arts and design, and architecture, I think, has, for instance, separated out against art at the beginning of this century and has become an autonomous discourse. And this means that it makes no sense any more to try to have a blueprint of a better society, or a different society, because it is no longer possible in a single vision to integrate all these autonomous discourses. And so, in a way, it is a kind of complexity barrier which prevents us, and we all feel it intuitively and we withdraw therefore and no longer engage with this kind of naive conception of inventing a better life. Nevertheless, I think some of the reactions have turned into a kind of a l'art-pour-l'art and self-serving formal games and that what's going on in architecture is often criticized and talked about as a kind of series of fashion cycles etc., but I think that's certainly not the case and it seems in Aarons remarks, that he is kind of... – there's an undercurrent of this kind of, let's say, criticism and misinterpretation – I would argue against kind of the architect's fetish objects, formal obsessions. Bart was arguing against – was bringing in the notion that urbanism is a domain, where the architect still has a kind of role to play and where it might be possible to have a kind of rationalistic, blueprint argument referring to MVRDV – and I think, I'm challenging this and argue that as part of a kind of evolutionary process, where a series of independent domains co-evolve, irritate each other, respond to each other, has replaced this kind of planned and blueprinted way of moving forward, yet we're moving in a certain direction, we're moving with degrees of inevitability also. I can just give a few examples, which might be more striking than recent architecture, for example the introduction of the mobile phone. It's been a kind of evolutionary shift or stage, which is absolutely impossible to step back from. To just say it's kind of – because, society all over in ways of communication and work and a certain material level of efficiency in reproduction cycles has been achieved by this, which makes it absolutely impossible to cut that out. So we have a series of innovations, to pick up on Michael Speaks' term, which I think are also operating with what is going on in architecture – the appropriation and, at the moment of course, the play for engagement of new design media, moving on like Neil Leach rightly said into the challenge of how these technologies become fabrication-systems, have a similar kind of edge of inevitability, I would argue. Of course, it could be pushed in various directions, but I think I like a lot the notion of – Greg sticks in my mind – where, you know some people might look at the stuff and say: I mean, what, are you kind of wilfully and self-absorbedly playing with these forms and you are standing back and saying: no, these are not my forms, these are our forms, these are forms, which are proliferating inevitably, everybody is working on them. Industrial design is full of it and so we all have to take that on in a way and that is maybe also not true, because this could be pushed in various directions, but I do believe, that there is an inevitability, that these, like the mobile phone, these new production systems will come, these new product-chains will come, mass customization will replace mass production and the other paradigm we are working on right

now in a series of other installations like the AADRL-research with embedding intelligence systems, the kind of computing powers, which are easily available now into responsive, interactive, robotic environments – seems to be an absolutely inevitable, irresistible opportunity and once we realize, how readily available modelling tools are, with 3D-Max and MAYA to model and anticipate these kinds of intelligent systems and you see in the exhibition a series of examples there – this is so powerful, this is so – this will run through and has to be worked on and so I think, there is definitely a kind of interesting dialectic we have to discuss about the degrees of inevitability and the action, which is still to be taken. How is it shaped, how does it move forward? Once it is stated, and that's what I would say, it becomes inevitability. But then it was to be stated, wasn't something else, some other track could have embarked upon it, it's like a kind of ramifying tree. Once you've set signals, you've set down the row, it becomes irresistible. I think Greg is one of those, who has set a certain – who took certain routes down the branches and pulled the discipline along himself and everybody is now working on these issues he's put forward. That maybe wasn't inevitable, but once it was stated it has become so. Maybe I'll stop here.

KARI JORMAKKA

So, would you like to take up from there and in particular address the question – since you are one of the pioneers of the use of scientific and biological theories for the design purposes as well. So, do you see there – where do you see this inevitability? Do you see that there is a kind of scientific necessity? And where would you locate it? At what point of the design process will it then become this inevitable thing that legitimates itself?

GREG LYNN

I think there is a way to put both of your comments together, I mean, you know, that I can do that. I want to take a step back and say that it is not... – that none of this is necessarily about zeitgeist and non of this is theory logical. But if we broke down architectural thinking – like the kind of art conceptual work – I think you could break it down, you know, into saying that one could conceive if architecture is a service industry, which is probably our primary role in the end, which makes us different than even industrial design but very different than, you know, painting or graphic design or any other design field. So we are fortunately or unfortunately service professionals which means, that we have to have a certain voice, which is about responding to demands, satisfying requirements, dealing with complex situations, organizing them. Options of thinking of architecture outside of that service role is – you know definitely we can perform a critical function and this is where I don't want to say this is theory logical, but I mean if you look at the theoretical work done in the 70ies in Italy, in the 80ies in America and Europe, the critical position gave architecture a social, ideological role. Which was to critically respond to the service assumptions, try to intersect some kind of intellectual position against it. Now, you know the utopian position, which you know is another kind of voice for architecture, is not necessarily starting from the service economy and trying to be critical of it, but

Greg Lynn

Tom Verebes

actually trying to be provocative. And trying to do – trying to provoke social and cultural situations rather than critically reflect on them. OK, this is the dilemma and that is why I was nervous about the conference for more and more I think, that digital technology and this atmosphere of form has forced architecture into the position of being a provocative discipline. Right? So, you bring these new technologies in and they are automatically provocative in the urban environment, they are provocative of our field. But our intellectual and conceptional milieu is primarily critical. So I would just want to tease apart a critical intellectual position relative to ideology and culture from a provocative stance, which does not assume the, you know, the service industry component. So I think we are in a complex situation, where we came out of the 80ies, with a kind of dogma of criticality. You know, where you would be given a situation, you would automatically critically reflect on that situation, as a way of doing something new – and in come these digital technologies – you know, the two things I would be afraid of is just, you know, adopting a critical stance in a provocative field. That never works. The second thing is, I would not want to turn the provocative stance into just service industry, of ,what is the most expedient way we can build those things. Or what is the way that architecture turns these digital techniques into service industry, supply and demand? So for me, that's the dilemma we are in. We are not very good at being a provocative discourse, like we are not very good at being utopian in the end. Like making proposals about social and cultural arrangements. We are very good at being critical. And we are very good at being service professionals. But we are not provocative – we are not a provocative field. At least we haven't been in the recent past. So I think that is the way I would put both of your comments together and try to think this problem through.

KARI JORMAKKA
Tom, would you like to respond to that and situate your own practice into this trichotomy of provocation, criticality and service?

TOM VEREBES
I may first say, that the question of what it is that – who do we serve, and perhaps the nature of what it is that we do as a field, the question of multidisciplinarity in relation to maybe what Michael Speaks brought up this morning – earlier this morning – that we are not to necessarily be problem solving in the contemporary sense but we are out to produce innovation, if anything that does... – can you hear me in the other space?

BART LOOTSMA
Yes, but it seems as if you can't hear us, is this correct?

TOM VEREBES
Now I hear you. But it is you, who is supposed to hear us.

BART LOOTSMA
Carry on, but we will try to get to this place after your intervention... somehow there seems to be a delay in the technology, so it is difficult to immediately react or get into...

TOM VEREBES
If we are caught in an engagement of a question between being critical and being provocative, I think it is a question of who is it – what is the role that we have. And if anything that can unify any of the participants, are they in a conference or an exhibition such as this, is that perhaps a commitment to innovation rather than problem solving. I think it's been really put very well by Michael Speaks this morning. Also discussed were the questions of practice and experimentation. And perhaps the issues of responsibility, of what our responsibility is. Some clients would possibly say in the most normative architectural sense, that responsibility is to deliver a product, which is everything but experimental and serves as a product. The industry that we are serving in a fully tested way. Well, in fact, if anything that builds in a kind of a latent defect, rather than a latent utopia, because inevitably what we produce then is stuff that is linked and tested to the past. And if we can define who our industry is, and rather what it is we do, to say that we are multidisciplinary as a kind of context culture, I think it would be ok in a way to define a current context in those terms, simply because that maybe goes back hundreds of years, as a model that I know is different from the kind of modernisms that were talked about by the moderators earlier, but if there is a way of redefining what is it that architects do in relation to Greg's comments about the techniques and tools or the kind of digital practice and how – what it is that architects do, if anything that the architects sort of being educated within this new, apparently new mode of practice, which is really not anything

necessarily new, where we are able to apply our practice, is in fields that are parallel and adjacent in the sense of using the same technologies. Architects turn into film-makers, graphic designers work on architecture. There is a relationship between interface design, branding, environmental branding. They are all kind of overlapping cross-overs which, I think, shift from multi-disciplinary work to actually – we are all in a similar kind of mode of production, yet we serve different industries that expect different kinds of products. And in a way that addresses perhaps Patrik's concerns of a sort of distributed nature of – maybe I can paraphrase some of the issues you described – the questions in terms of these technologies that we use and who it is that we serve, the issues of interactivity. It is first here the question of interface, what is the interface of design, are they generatively or communicatively, you know, that the possibility of being able to work with people in the distributed sense, to work on projects in distant places, which is also a cliché at this point, it certainly is – it has become more of a reality than it ever was with groups such as CIAM or Team Ten or in any way the kind of modernist networks, that were formed ages ago. But then the kind of specific product, that we talked about as a kind of responsive or interactive – I think there are ways of engaging with – looking at material organization that is not mutual aesthetics, which does not simply imply a kind of kinetics or a reflexive response, but in the design process there is a way, let's say of charging and already installing a kind of generic as a resilience specific set of conditions rather than one that needs the feed-back of its users, but already installs and charges reciprocity between users and the specific interface of architecture. So maybe, just in some – the shifting ways in which we practice are partly in how we communicate, partly in the ways in which we design. The tools that we use and the fact that those are shared tools, and if anything are stolen or borrowed from other disciplines, from MAYA or Studio-Max, being primarily the animation and film tools. And that, I think, immediately sets our entire current mode of production into questioning: who is the client, what is the industry and what is it we are serving and are we limiting ourselves in who we serve and what we produce?

KARI JORMAKKA

Bart, before you can take over, let me ask just one question and let Marie Therese respond and explain her own...

PATRIK SCHUMACHER

I think, you should give over to the other space, before it drifts into a different orbit, a chance to talk.

KARI JORMAKKA

They'll have plenty of chance to talk, yet. I would just make one round and have Marie Therese explain – respond to the same question because I think that she represents a very different mode of practice. And I think that would be useful, this response...

MARIE THERESE HARNONCOURT

I will be very brief so that Bart doesn't get nervous over there. I just want to point out something. I think, there is something provocative going on in the architecture shown also in the exhibition, in the work that is presented, because there is a big longing for dealing with form and shaping space. And I think, if you look around at what is going on in building industry or in this direction, there is no place for space or thinking about space, anymore. It is all about function and how things work and about efficiency, and therefore I think, putting the stress on spatial quality and space which also can be used to provoke new programs again, and not thinking just about an installation or a house, even thinking about urban spaces, I think all these experiments are very important, and maybe we don't know where they will all end up, yet. We can not really put it into words now, but I think, there is a big potential, and we in our work are obsessed with this spatial power and I think, this is something we also should talk about, because I think, other positions are also thinking that there is a potential in this way.

KARI JORMAKKA

So Bart, we are all waiting to see how you respond to that.

BART LOOTSMA

So well, you may be – I mean, actually the appearance of an upper world and an underworld is a very classical theme of utopias. But the underworld is always deprived, which you see in Metropolis of Fritz Lang and in other utopias. Anyway, and it's always that the ones, that are down in the underworld, are a bit less privileged, so

we are getting a bit nervous here, but indeed you would be surprised, but we do have a group of people here as well, that I would like to introduce very quickly, and that is starting here with Michael Hensel that you don't see, but he's here, we also see Kivi Sotamaa and Michael Hensel from ocean NORTH, then you see already Hani Rashid from asymptote, Oliver Salway from Softroom and Hannes Traupmann and Christoph Pichler from Pichler & Traupmann.

So, we have been listening to what you have been saying and as it is written in the small brochure, this panel is supposed to be much more about urbanism and urban spaces. Actually that relates in quite an interesting way to what we have been hearing up to now, particularly when I think of what Greg said about architecture being a service industry, and then the role of the utopian position. What strikes me is, that somehow the scale or the issue of urbanism is completely lacking, and also what strikes me is that, let's say, a European tradition is missing in what you all are saying. I would say that in Europe, architecture is largely embedded in urbanism and therefore in politics. Now you may ask if these are utopian politics but at least, there is a constant relation to it. It is not so much an industry, of course it has some characteristics of an industry as well, but it's relation to politics seems to be much stronger as soon as you talk about cities and urbanism.

Well, maybe to start with Hani, because in a kind of... to make a link to Greg: What role would urbanism play in this respect, talking about utopia and talking about a particular kind of architecture as it is presented in this exhibition?

GREG LYNN

Hey Bart, why are you pitting Europeans against the Americans? And just out of curiosity: are you saying when an American architect builds in Europe, is that a more urban or political thing? Or are you saying, that this is something about the architects or the context or both? 'Cause all the European architects I know are building in America, and all the Americans I know are building in Europe. So it is going to be tough to sort this out.

BART LOOTSMA

Well, that is for the kind of circle of architects you are working with, but for the average European and American architect this would not be the case. But what starts to strike me in the architectural debate of the last couple of years is really this difference of, on the one hand, talking about, like you do, architecture as a service industry, while in Europe there is much more a tradition that comes from public housing, from urban planning, etc., that is really politically and bureaucratically embedded. I miss that when I hear the different positions in your panel, I somehow miss that position. Because even if this is a very pragmatic position or a kind of way in which architecture and urbanism are related to the welfare state, that opens the way to have a kind of ideological, political debate that might open up to a kind of utopian position. At least these are some kind of different aspects to the debate. Hani?

HANI RASHID

Well that's interesting because I think that in some senses it might be an American import, in the sense of a sort of pragmatic urgency, like Greg was saying. The incredible thing is that with the post war modernist architecture, we have fallen into a continuous cycle of style and methodologies, movements and tendencies, we have played a kind of dilettante role architecturally and artistically for a long time. The question really on the floor is: is there a kind of urgency today, that takes a sort of experimentation as we have seen at the show, in a sort of fantastic kind of possibilities, that the digitals are allowing us and procedures are allowing us. And sensing what in fact is that sense of urgency that will promote or prompt us to start to put some really compelling and powerful positions into the mix. In other words rather than just looking dangerously at something like what is at the show here and what is shown in other different places as, yet, other attempts of style, other kinds of free formed experiment – it is really kind of isolating the particular sort of human and technological concerns that are the root of all of this. There is something in Greg's discourse as I understand it, especially lately – but I think it's really kind of critical to the issues, the sense of really being a generation of architects that in fact has no kind of restrictions like any other generation of architects had, and these technologies allow a kind of versatility and language and ability to use this and provoke in interesting ways and that ties all the way from representation to manufacturing possibilities and capabilities and ultimately to a kind of producing. Perhaps not utopias again, because we are shell-shocked by the European utopias of the post-war era. And therefore in a kind of American tradition, let's say, there has been a quite pragmatic approach to these problems. My question, really, Greg, and to the panel is: "where are the critical points and actual spaces in which we as architects need to operate today, that do not produce yet another style or another dogma, and definitely do not produce yet another sort of depraved utopianism that we kind of battle to the world from our position?" And I think that a lot of that has to do with what we see in the show and what we see upstairs, but lingering beneath all the works – be they purely phenomenological, experimental and kind of very far away from potential building proposition, or be they in fact in the most sort of pragmatic explorations of technique and building. Lingering beneath all of that are some very, very interesting and critical issues moving forward for architects. That kind of stops something generationally and stylistically and finally I feel that there is a possibility to move on. So the question is, where are those positions across the board. I'm very interested in hearing about that – from Kivi for example.

Continued on page 81

Interviews 2

Eva Grubbauer

First I would like to get an impression of the way you work and the way you think. How would you characterize your work, where is the difference to other architects and what is your most characteristic project?

Greg Lynn

Well, it is tough for me to talk about anything else but the WTC-competition that I am doing with offices like UN Studio, Foreign Office Architects, Reiser Umemoto and so on. This is a generation of people who have all been close

colleagues, who have all been competing against one and another and who have a lot of similarities. But for this collaboration we are trying to figure out what the differences are, so that everybody can do a distinct job. My particular expertise is clearly in both, form making and making a conceptual argument about particular forms. My role within the competition is to help focus the conceptual approach in terms of metaphysics, culture and history. And I also have computer skills – that's maybe more important.

Eva Grubbauer

How important is your personal background and your education for your work?

Greg Lynn

It's probably everything. My background in philosophy and my decision to go to a graduate school where there was a strong history and theory faculty, those experiences inevitably shaped my interests. And probably because of how I was educated, I was always trying to connect my work with historical trajectory and to theorize my work.

Greg Lynn
Greg Lynn FORM

Eva Grubbauer

How important is the place, where you are doing a project?

Greg Lynn

The location is always very important. Probably my reflex is to go to typology first and then to go to the location. Then I try to draw out some architectural response to the context, to hook the architecture into some familiar, local reference. But I don't think I will ever have the regional style because right now our work is all over the place. We're doing a project in the jungle of Costa Rica, we are doing a housing-job in the Netherlands, we are doing this World Trade Center competition and there is no logic to those places.

I think, in architecture there is a little bit of a crisis right now because the firms that are driving the discourse are at the same time very regional, like Glenn Murcutt and very modern, like Jaques Herzog or Rem Koolhaas. Herzog is very Swiss in his vocabulary but you couldn't really say that he is a regional architect. The same with Koolhaas: he is a modern architect but also very Dutch. So, everybody is making modern architecture homey, warm and fuzzy and in that sense there is a possibility, that someone like Glenn Murcutt is a modernist, but he is also an Australian modernist and Herzog is a Swiss modernist and Rem is a Dutch modernist. But I, for myself,

don't really feel like I've got a Los Angeles or an American style, but I just may be too close to it.

Eva Grubbauer

For us in Europe it seems that in the United States theory and building – the real construction firms – are separated. It appears that there is some architecture which is very sophisticated, but in general the whole mass is built by companies.

Greg Lynn

If you look at the country, you are right. If you go to New York City and you want to see contemporary architecture, it's very difficult. It's very easy to go to a university or a museum in New York and see exhibitions of contemporary architecture, probably easier than in any other place of the world, but if one of my students of the "Angewandte" is coming to New York and he wants to see new architecture, you could send him to four or five places. But the place you would send him is actually a place like Ohio, with their four Frank Gehry buildings, a Zaha Hadid building, a Wolf Prix building, a mix of American and European architects who work theoretical and progressive. America has a lot of architecture being built, it's just not where one expects the capital of American culture. If you go to Minneapolis, Ohio, Los Angeles, there is a lot of interesting new

architecture, where theorists are also building, but if you go to Boston, Washington D.C., New York, San Francisco – nothing. There are one or two things but not a lot. It's more on the margins of Americas big cities you get interesting architecture but not in the centre. That is different from Europe. Here the margins are very conservative and the centres are progressive, in the United States it's exactly reverse.

Eva Grubbauer

How long do you stay with a project? Do you go to the construction site, look at what is happening and draw details or is this something you leave to other teams?

Greg Lynn

Because of the complexity of the forms that we design, we can't turn over the details to somebody else even if we wanted to. So, in that sense we are involved basically in an equal proportion through the whole project. For the project in the Netherlands, for example, I don't know the course of construction in the Netherlands, I don't know about building laws in the Netherlands, I don't know about consultants in the Netherlands, so the very beginning of the project I am turning over maybe 40 to 60% of the project to someone local who knows the situation. But when it's time to build the project, they don't know how to build our forms, so we have to keep doing 40 to 60% of the working drawings. So, unlike the 1970ies and 80ies, when an architect like me could do 100% of the design and turn over 100% of the construction to a local office, now it is much more of an even balanced through the whole sequence.

Eva Grubbauer

When do you decide the materials? Is there a difference between your drawings and the final construction?

Greg Lynn

As a young architect I was in a strange situation because I got a large project that I started my office with – this church in New York. So, when most young architects do small-scaled projects and work up to large-scaled projects, usually the first thing they do is develop a palette of materials for an interior architecture, then a palette for an exterior domestic architecture – a shop or something – and then they work up in scale. For me with a large-scale project, the research didn't start in terms of materials.

I became aware of this almost three years ago when I took this interior design project in Stockholm, Sweden. The project itself was not so interesting but it was an opportunity to explore a palette of materials and since that time we have consistently done one interior a year and we're developing a palette of materials. But it's a kind of strange palette because we do formed plastics, we're doing a lot with shaping-foam, we're working with hard-woods, corks and light-weight-cast-concrete. So those are mostly materials that come out of the automobile-industry and the boat industry rather than from the furniture- and construction industry. We now have a kind of house-library of materials and we also bought a big CNC-mill that is in the office, so we can build furniture and wall-panels and even exterior mock-ups in the office and then take it to a contractor and show them what to do.

Elisabeth Nöst-Kahlen
I would like to welcome
Christoph Pichler and Hannes
Traupmann and my first question is:
How would you characterize your
architecture, what are the most
important aspects and how does it
differ from the work of other
architects?

Christoph Pichler
An important feature in our
kind of architecture is dealing with
dualities, which can be taken both
from completely simple life and

Christoph Pichler, Hannes Traupmann
Pichler & Traupmann

from areas specific to architecture. Such dualities might, for instance, be light and heavy or life and death. The second important theme in our work is continuity, although this may seem to contrast with the concept of duality. Our aim, however, is to take this contradiction into an area of tension where we then position our architecture.

Hannes Traupmann

Often it is all about the nature, that is to say the essence, of things; we intentionally adopt a critical approach to the concepts, trying to fathom out ontological shifts and implementing them in corresponding architectural issues. A concrete example would be our installation for the "Latent Utopias" exhibition, i.e. the concept of room door or door room, toying with ambiguity, which is not one that can be misunderstood, but which leaves a large space between the two poles of tension.

Christoph Pichler

Some things happen simultaneously: something can be open and closed at the same time; upon opening one thing, I might shut off another path – this happens in our object by making several statuses happen at the same time, so that we free it from exclusivity. In our buildings, too, inside and outside can take place at the very same time – there is no longer a separation.

Hannes Traupmann

You also asked about how we are different from our colleagues. I would like to highlight in this context that we do not work on specific forms, as we have heard the term 'form' frequently during the symposium and it was chiefly about instrumentalising statuses and behavior patterns. So for us it is essential to find out what can be left out in order to create space. We aim for an area of tension and in between to keep something open for the interactive part. This is what we really perceive as architecture, and I believe this is what makes us essentially different from other offices.

Elisabeth Nöst-Kahlen

How important is 3D visualization for you? Is the computer a means to an end or does it have an influence on your architecture?

Hannes Traupmann

The computer is simply a tool for us. Of course we can see the undeniable possibilities of the tool as a design-generating instrument; however, for us it is not so important or at least, not yet. I do not know how this is going to develop, but our analysis is currently running on a different level.

Christoph Pichler

I'm afraid that colleagues who have staked their claim

unfortunately also use the computer mainly as an object or mechanism for representation. Forms that cannot easily be realized manually or with a model are now implemented with the help of the computer. However, these forms are only the representation of contents and I see the greatest challenge in finding a simple implementation into factual reality for complex content. I do not want to simulate interaction via a complex loop, but rather produce an interaction with a very simple element – a wall, a slab etc. We are very aware of the theoretical background, especially since I observed the same development in 1990/91 in the USA. Still, I asked myself, what should I do with this theory? Can it really have any influence on our simple everyday space or does digitalization only serve the production of complex images?

Hannes Traupmann

That's the right keyword: can the medium be used in a way that space is realized and not just virtualised? And this is, as we said before, our contribution to "Latent Utopias" – a space we generated as an exhibition object. By implanting an object that again is a space that really does exist, not just potentially could be.

Elisabeth Nöst-Kahlen

To what extent does your cultural background influence your architecture? Earlier, you talked about life and death; I read that one of you studied theology...

Hannes Traupmann

That was me. I think it would be too superficial to think that all reflection is based on the templates of life and death and that these would be the essential contents of religion and theology. I believe that in our reception we tend instead to proceed phenomenologically and stick to a reality concept, not just a virtuality concept. And one of the most significant images of reality is indeed duality. Of course, we did not invent them; they have existed ever since there has been reality, which is not necessarily connected with my theology studies. It might have some anonymous influence, but I don't want to make it a topic from this standpoint; however, I like to do so as an architect.

Elisabeth Nöst-Kahlen

What meaning does the site you are building on have for you?

Christoph Pichler

We think that architecture cannot be separated from the place or site for which it is conceived or in which it will take place. We do not believe in the UFO that can fly in from anywhere and set itself down. Instead, we believe in the fact that the place is there first of all and will influence the object that will be there. First of all, there will be an interaction between what was there previously – landscape, town and programme - and an idea, which is then added. The object, and this also applies for our contribution to the exhibition, can only take place in a certain place and is totally useless if taken away from there.

Elisabeth Nöst-Kahlen

How do you judge the mutual influence of teaching activities and practical work in your case?

Hannes Traupmann

I try to convey a basic attitude, which is of course determined by the thoughts that occupy us in our practical work. Of course students are free to deal with this in whatever way they want.

Christoph Pichler

It would be tricky for me to place my reflections vis-à-vis those of the students. From my own attempts every day to implement ideas in practice, I am aware how difficult it is. Often it is only a very small percentage of the total mass of thoughts that really influence the concrete object. This makes us more self-critical than we would be if we remained within the space of theory and pure concepts.

Farshid Moussavi, Alejandro Zaera Polo
Foreign Office Architects

and we are very interested in how they integrate within the project. For the Yokohama-project, for example, we did all the drawings.

Eva Grubbauer
In your own office?

Farshid Moussavi
Yes, I think that continuity is very important and so we had a site office with our own people and even when the contractors were doing drawings they showed it to us five times to be checked, before they were approved for construction.

Eva Grubbauer
Talking about the Yokohama-project: When did you start thinking about the materials?

Farshid Moussavi
The basic material, which was steel, was decided at the beginning because that really dictated the kind of structure one would design. But the finishes were settled much later.

Alejandro Zaera Polo
Anyway, we thought about the finishes during the competition stage but we changed that all.

Eva Grubbauer
Because of the budget?

Alejandro Zaera Polo
No, because in the development of the project we

Eva Grubbauer
How would you characterize your work and which project would you present to characterize yourself?

Farshid Moussavi
I guess, the project, that we are best known for is the Yokohama-Port-Terminal–project that we won as a competition and have recently completed.

We are very interested in different processes that one has to embrace to produce a piece of architecture. That doesn't mean just an initial conception of the project but also the way through its construction. It is about how to incorporate and how to transfer problems and information into form. There are many different scales that you need to address at various moments along a building process realized, that it would make more sense to change the finishes. We don't think that one has to be faithful to any original idea. He has to exploit the opportunities that appear through the process. So if there is a more interesting material that appears halfway through the process, we throw it over.

Farshid Moussavi

It is important that you are open to all the different input that is given to you from the client or your own imagination or people in your office or the contractors or the politicians, so that you can actually bring in as much intelligence to the project as possible.

Eva Grubbauer

How important is your personal and cultural background? Your name – Foreign Office Architects – tells us, that you are not working in the country where you are from. How important is this?

Alejandro Zaera Polo

It is important although it's probably something that happens to almost everybody to some degree. The idea of Foreign Office came out of realizing that we had a certain power because of our cultural alienation.

Eva Grubbauer

Do you have more distance?

Alejandro Zaera Polo

Yes. That is a condition that most creative people need because in order to produce something new and innovative, you need to somehow place yourself outside the rules. Foreignness is one possibility to be an outsider and the idea of Foreign Office Architects was, that this condition of alienation is turning into a kind of productive moment for the practice.

Eva Grubbauer

When you have a new project in a new country – how do you deal with the situation?

Alejandro Zaera Polo

There are many people who think, that our work isn't contextual but that's not true. In fact I think, that we are extremely contextual but it's just that we look at the context in a different way

than a regular inhabitant might do. When you are a foreigner you tend to be more attentive to the environment because you are not in an environment where you know how things are going to happen. You may be more sensitive to the context than a local and I think, that's actually what is happening to us. We are always very interested in the local process of production, we always talk about making architecture in different countries like, for example, producing Cabernet Sauvignon in Nappa Valley. You take a certain technique that was elaborated upon in France, you take the grape and then you go to southern California.

Then you understand that the wine needs a certain slope of the hill, certain ground and certain weather and for some funny reason you produce the best Cabernet Sauvignon because there is also something in southern California, that gives to that grape a slightly different flavour. We think, that this operation is quite similar to the one that architects have to do. It is not about keeping the tradition of the wine in a certain location; you have

to be able to have the abstracted production-process in your mind and then search for locations that are adequate.

I also want to say that we don't like to design buildings, we like to "grow" buildings with the idea of going to a place and letting the materials that are there somehow inform the techniques of constructing the project.

Eva Grubbauer

Are you satisfied with the built result of the Yokohama-Port-terminal?

Farshid Moussavi

Yes. Obviously the process contained all sorts of compromises and changes but I think, that it has been completed in a successful way.

Alejandro Zaera Polo

I would say, that it is actually very rare, that a project of this size is allowed ever to take the amount of risk and the level of experimentation with the construction-technology, that this project has had.

Farshid Moussavi

Yes, but you also see the way people react to it. You know, you have all your experiments in structure and glazing etc. but ultimately, what you want to do is to give something new to the people and people were really reacting. It was something completely new for them. Suddenly they were "foreigners" in their own country and they didn't know whether they should sit somewhere or stand somewhere or sleep somewhere. For them the spaces were not dictated and after a while you could see that people were taking their own risk, if you like. They were going up to places where maybe they really shouldn't and for me that was a huge success.

Eva Grubbauer

You also teach – how does your work influence your teaching and vice versa?

Alejandro Zaera Polo

It is obviously connected. Our practice is a kind of practice that emerges somehow from the engagement in the academic milieu. Many of the people who work for us have been our students which means, that we had the chance to form a very close ideological bond to them. This is a very luxurious condition if you compare it with corporate offices where they just buy people. Our academic engagement, no matter how heavy it becomes sometimes in terms of time-commitments and things like that, gives us the chance to construct a team that is ideologically consistent and that gives us an enormous power. It also teaches you to articulate your ideas. So, we are not just making architecture, we are also creating architectural knowledge because of our teaching background.

The third thing is, that teaching allows you to test things that you sometimes cannot test in practice because of many constraints, which you don't have or which you can look at positively in the academic environment.

End of
Interviews 2

Space condition part 1 continued from page 64

KIVI SOTAMAA

To come to this question about how the form-experiment might relate to the urban environment: It is quite interesting to see how a certain branch of architecture somehow has changed its disciplinary filiation, so to speak, from let's say Baukunst and engineering and applied philosophy to say a search for more operational models in biology for instance, looking for possibilities in ecological models, where you could say: "how does a species relate to a larger environment. How does a formal experiment relate to an urban environment?" Plainly speaking you will also then have to acknowledge, that these kind of experiments, to use the term from earlier on, are probably best conducted in public spaces, because there you get an undetermined response to your intervention. So it is actually quite interesting to see, that this issue of latency, the kind of bridge between the NOW and the NEXT can really be done in the experiment, in the insertion of the formal experiment into the city. And I think, there would be something quite interesting to discuss, what kind of models underlie that and by what are they facilitated? Because so far a lot of the discussion at least within the panel goes up to the point of finishing and completing the design of the object etc., you may call it building, you may call it a certain public space. But there is then life that actually begins to merge already and only at that moment of the insertion, where observational techniques are very important, where we have to register how, in fact, these forms are used. And it would actually really be fantastic to have video cameras, in fact there are surveillance cameras in the exhibition space, to see whether this can already be indicative of a certain urban space of this determination, why these kind of forms and why people will in some way or another react with these kinds of forms. Unfortunately most of the exhibition strategies are still more a celebration of the pristine object, rather than the placement in a kind of emergent social arrangement, I would say.

BART LOOTSMA

Hannes, may I ask you to react to this. I mean how do you see yourself in this aspect and do you feel yourself as being a part of this surface-industry or do you feel yourself being in a kind of different tradition than that.

HANNES TRAUPMANN

I think, the word utopia provokes a great idea and through history, when looking at things that deal with utopia – I think it's a great idea, when somebody wants to put it into society or into life – anyway, and now more or less I have the feeling, that architecture doesn't have any great idea in that sense. It's more a kind of a reaction to what's going on around, to what's happening, especially coming from physical matters or coming from biology as you said, and more or less, the architecture tries to react to these systems and is trying to give a kind of "Abbildung". It's a kind of

representation of what is already found and what
is already seen in other disciplines and I am really
trying to find out, even from this exhibition, what
could be the thing that would really change the
material, what could really change society,
because, I mean since I heard these important
words "the philosophers knew how to interpret
the reality but we are going to change it", I'd really
ask this very important question and I think it
could only be done if we found an instrument, that
could change the space and does not just react to
something.

BART LOOTSMA

Thank you. I would ask you to explain this
idea about let's say examples from biology,
physics, etc. that seem to be very present in this
whole exhibition. In terms of let's say going to bed
with utopia – maybe I'll read the words with which
I end my contribution in the catalogue from Colin
Bird, who wrote a book of liberal individualism,
and we are somehow in a kind of spirit of the time,
that we think that liberal individualism is not a
system – anyway, Colin Bird writes: "I can believe,
that the state is really an organism and yet deny
that it has any moral significance whatsoever. In
fact, that a jellyfish is organic it is not elevated to a
moral status equivalent to or beyond that of a
human being. Similarly, I can't deny that
collectivities or states are in any sense organic or
anthropomorphic and yet claim that they have a
greater claim on our moral attention than mere
human individuals." May I bounce that back to
the other panel?

Kivi Sotamaa

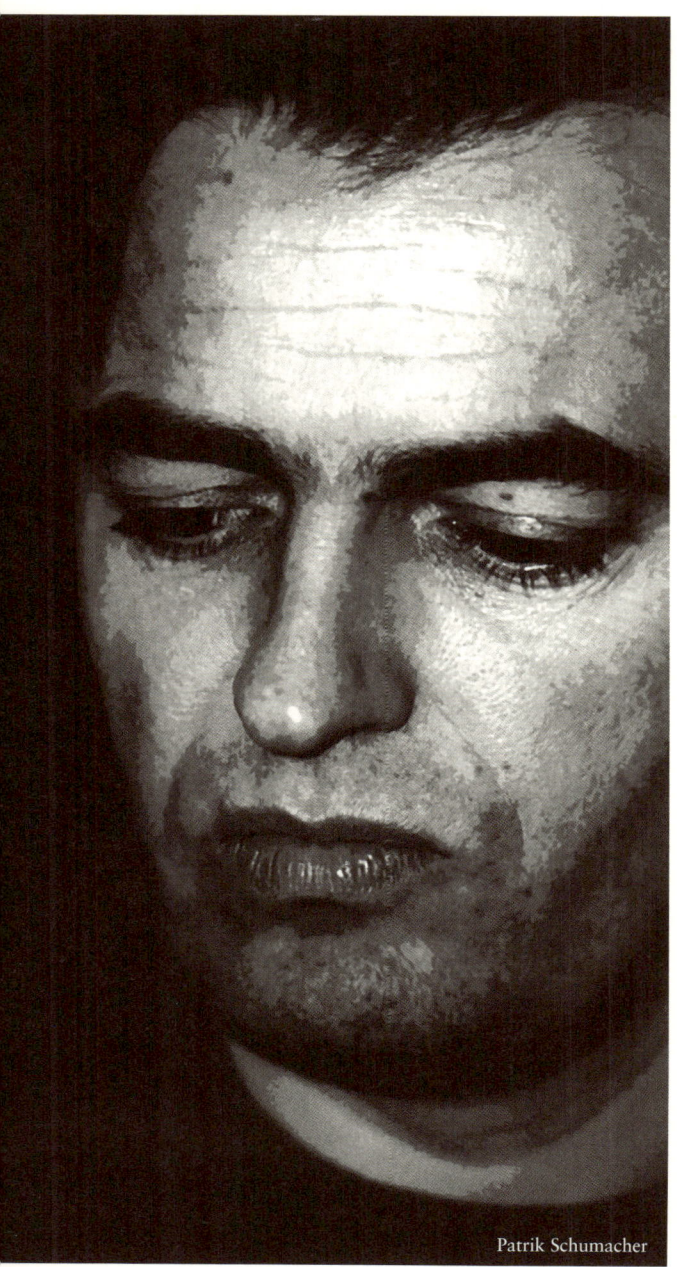

Patrik Schumacher

KARI JORMAKKA

You may, but I don't think anybody heard what you said, this is the problem, but I think that you were saying something about this constitution of an ethic which is based on something other than a human being. So I think, that's a very appropriate question and we should come back to this and I would really like to come back perhaps to Patrik, as well as to Greg and this issue of trying to find an alternative thesis, whether it is found in biological or social organizations or such things. I would just want to make the point that what you said about inevitability is of course, in a certain sense, already implied by the name of the exhibition – in the sense that, when we talk about latent utopias, it is in a way – when we say it is "latent" we imply it is inherent – it's already there, it is already inevitable – thereby we use that manner of argumentation as a way of taking a moral responsibility overt thought. Perhaps you could take it from there?

PATRIK SCHUMACHER

Well I have to come in and say, that of course, inevitability is much too strong, I have to immediately take that back. This is a kind of arbitrariness, a kind of 'anything-goes', an individual kind of fancy. There is something in between. As I said it is only inevitable, after a certain thing has been shown and establishes a new level – let's say what Luhmann calls, an evolutionary achievement, which we become materially dependent upon and we can not longer step back from. And we know that the electronic revolution has achieved that and that we are absolutely dependent on these systems and that we'd have a catastrophe, if some of these systems disintegrated. Even the device of the mobile phone can no longer be withdrawn. But I want to come back to your question about the ethics, which might be inherent or which might come along with the new evolutionary level of technology, but it is not, of course, always technology, but I would say it's always a kind of synthesis or co-evolution of a new level of technological devices and techniques and the social arrangements and communication processes and the social differentiations which come along with that. It is always the symbiosis of technology and social relations, which establishes levels in the evolutionary process. And I think that some of the ethics I have been pointing to were already mentioned in terms of the autpoiesis of different domains within the overall social process. As you said, everybody knows by now, that the sciences can only define their own criteria of truth obviously, of validity, but also of what is a valid or worthwhile research agenda. There is very little interference. At the same time of course, this system of self-reproduction has to watch out that it remains relevant and gives back and has to watch politics and has to watch economics and has to watch, let's say family-relations and the every day life systems, to find it's research agendas. But it's finding itself. In the reverse course also for economics. Economic has its own logic, has its own agenda, but is watching very carefully, is on the alert. And I think, architecture in a similar way, we are highly sensitive to what is going on in the economic domain, in the political

domain, but it is our business – we don't have politicians that tell us, we don't have economists that tell us – in this sense we are not in the situation that the client could tell us, because he doesn't know either. He just knows how to calculate, maybe how to set up new models of economic implementation, but he does not know what he is supposed to implement, there he depends on us. So in this kind of series of co-evolving autocratic systems, they have their own logic, their own categories of discourse, and they are kind of semi-independent, they define their own agendas, but they are watching us very carefully and they are reacting to each other. Therefore this kind of dialectic of acting or reacting is also dissolved, because it's both: as I react, I already misinterpret and act upon somebody else who has to follow. This kind of passing the ball around is always a kind of double-edged sword. And I think, in terms of the ethics – Koolhaas was very sensitive to that – you know the alertness, the delay and the suspensions of moral judgment, a kind of excessive tolerance on the one hand, while at the same time a kind of critical alertness, of what to pick up on. These are elements of a new ethics, which is how we are dealing with this kind of post-blueprint era, this kind of knew level of complexity in the social process and that we should reflect upon. And I think intuitively we already act upon these ethics, because if we didn't, we would just be stumbling like an elephant in the glass-house and those, who make careers are themselves within that new ethic.

KARI JORMAKKA

Ok, can I take the question to the other panel. But I'd reformulate it slightly from what you said in the sense that if we take science as a kind of domain in and of itself, which defines its own criteria and values and so on, its own conditions as it were. I can somehow in my mind imagine, that architecture can aspire to that condition, I can't imagine that urbanism would. And so, could there be an urbanism as this kind of a discourse that sets its own agenda and its own criteria? Could there even be that kind of architecture? Back to you.

BART LOOTSMA

Yes, that is a very interesting question, but one of the things that strikes me here is that we talk about architecture as a discipline and it seems to me now, the question is almost as if urbanism is also a discipline, that somehow works by itself. Probably just like architecture needs commissions even though you can make all kinds of plans without a commission, I have got the feeling, that urbanism is much more embedded in the political process in society. But maybe I should ask Kivi to react to this. The question is, wether urbanism has more chances to intervene on this ethical kind of level?

KIVI SOTAMAA

To be honest, I have difficulty relating to the discourse, so I will do a very simple thing. There is something and I think I picked it up from Greg's comment a while back. Greg talked about architecture as service and provocation and I

can't help thinking: Isn't it specifically in a relation to public space, isn't it one of the functions of architecture to be provocative? Isn't it one of the services that architecture should provide? It is a lot of discussion, but the general approach in architectural design or urban design has to do with functions, customization, customer needs, trying to map and understand dynamic forces in a better way. But what I find most exciting about contemporary cities or contemporary public spaces, which are the themes of this panel, as far as I understood, is the fact, that these spaces are spaces of conflict. They are heterogeneous, they are changing, they are unpredictable. And I think, design for this kind of – for the contemporary urban city, has to take a slightly different approach. I think one of the services that the architecture has to provide is, that it should provoke social encounter. It should give people the possibility to discover and require them at the same time to adapt, actually. It is not for the discussion – certainly the architectural design a lot of time talks about – it's kind of one way – I think actually architecture relates to art also in that sense. In a lot of our work, we have an attitude – well it's difficult, or we take an attitude, where we actually try to provoke and enable things to go a way beyond the particular brief or the particular requirements of the projects. This is very badly formulated but... well Greg, maybe if you understand what I mean, can you react to this?

GREG LYNN

I don't know. I sympathize with you. There is a reflex, maybe it's architectural, maybe it is more than that, a reflex to look out at exactly the time when you should be looking into your own field and for me, I think this is the question of the conflict of the discipline versus the context, and so I am as guilty of it as anybody, but I started looking at scientific models of organization. Not to justify, but actually to focus what was already happening in architecture, and when I would go to a conference, that wasn't an architectural conference, like saying an automobile designer's conference, you would walk in and they would say, "we are so excited to talk to somebody, who can deal with large assemblies of parts, that are all unified to make an object and are always mass-produced in one way or another and sometimes are kits of parts. And there is an architectural intelligence, that we invited you to this conference for", and I realized that everything I was looking out to scientific models for, people not in architecture were already looking in our field for the expertise. And that's the problem of taking a provocative discipline and running it through a critical discourse. To be just very crass, it is not that simple, but a critical position in terms of context and discipline is always going to look outside the discipline and back in terms of the context. So, if you show it to a critical intelligence, maybe Frederic Kiesler and it makes it into a stylistic critical argument versus if you show it to somebody who is more of the utopian, let's say, they look forward in terms of the context, like what can this do and they look deeper into the field, in terms of how are you going to do it and what is the intelligence of your field. It's going to make some future context possible. So for me it's, you know, when you take a new approach, which is coming from inside the field and you run it through a critical grinder, you end up getting in these conflicted situations.

PATRIK SCHUMACHER

But I think, it is a very useful distinction and – discipline versus context which matches my system theoretical difference between the system and its environment and somehow the discipline as a system engages within the environment through a certain kind of boundary maintenance and cross communication I think, so the discipline itself differentiates to a certain extent into those, which are watching out for what is going on and whether architecture, what the discipline produces, is relevant. And those are the critiques to a certain extent. People like Bart Lootsma obviously and some others start to specialize in that kind of boundary policing or filtration process between the discipline and its context. Doing research on the context, with the eye of... being on alert to what becomes relevant for architecture and also testing architecture with respect of its context. And I think, this is very healthy and it is also very healthy that those, who are working on the internal mechanisms of the discipline, are shielded from instant and simultaneous addressing of the context and all it's aspects. So I think it is extremely important that the discipline has its internal differentiation and that to a certain extent arbitrarily and accidentally this became American versus Dutch. American, which aggressively, with Kipnis, Eisenman and Greg in a sense, stating the fact. I think it is a truth which comes from "lived experience", that you have to cut out a lot of issues, a lot of claims, "a gun to your head": Tell me what this means, tell me what this is for, tell me how and why is that! You have to back off from this in order to allow a kind of internal processing of form and material, which has, and that is very important, already gone through an evolution, where it has a number of cycles of being... – having been relevant and working in society. And you take the formal substratum – it is not pure form, it is the formal aspects of the living organism of architecture and society, which you take with it's formal aspects and you derive its formal aspects, and you proliferate a series of new formal options and then the critics can come in and poke their noses in. But they have to let, and this is a new kind of level of ethics within the discipline, they have to let these guys, the formal researchers, do their work to have something to criticize. Because otherwise, you keep looking at an empty sheet, where the first three lines are always criticized out of existence. And I think "Latent Utopias" is that, too. And I think also, it is not only for the critics, it is for the audiences, and that is why it has to become a public event and a kind of – like art does it for..., like the electronic media for a number of other film..., etc, similar kind of experimental chamber and then throwing it out, because this process of criticism is done by the critics and they are very much tied up with other disciplines, with other demands of the general population. I think this is extremely important to realize, that this is an overall disciplinary organism, which works...

KARI JORMAKKA

But I wonder if there is a discipline really? I think that one of the things we see in the work which is presented in the exhibition is really this questioning of the discipline and the expansion of the discipline to various directions. If one thinks that the utopian potential, or any potential for any new experimentation or whatever, comes from within the system rather than from the environment as such. I just wonder, how big is the system then? Is it one project or do we really have to postulate the existence of urbanism as a discipline and architecture as a discipline. And I would pose one question simply in this context, which is, I think Xavier Costa in the first session referred to, just like what Greg was talking about, pitying Americans as contrasted with Europeans, he made this dichotomy of pragmatism versus utopia. Whether utopia seems to be really this internal discourse, which has a certain potential and pragmatism, which is then working in a very different way, I think that this dichotomy is also a challenge and I would actually throw this question back at anybody who cares to answer it. Is it really so, that we have pragmatism versus utopia. At least if we think about this in terms of philosophy, pragmatic philosophy, then it would seem like, it would be very easy to combine pragmatism and philosophy, pragmatism and utopia, because you would involve basic necessities and inevitabilities and things like that into this questioning.

HANI RASHID

I was in the city of Singapore with the planning department three weeks ago, and they took me to a room, I do not know if any of you have had the chance to see it, but they have a room the size of this room here, which is a model of Singapore and it's future plans and it is the most obscene model you can imagine as an architectural fetishist. It is just one skyscraper after another – endless, it is incredible. And they took a laser pointer out and they said: "over there that's KPF, and over there it is SOM", and I was just kind of..., could not believe this. It was fantastic, just imagine I pointed at all your heads and claimed you were all skyscrapers. So we started a discussion and I got the chance to speak with them about our work and showed them some of the work of people in this show. And at the end of the discussion the question was: "What can you do for us then? How can you engage us as a real client?" And I said: "Are you actually interested in becoming our client, because, I mean, how can we go ahead with that?" So we started a project with them, where we are doing a master planning scenario, let's say, but we are employing a lot of the techniques that are in this show, a lot of digital mechanisms and tools and automatic tools and data-scaping tools to produce a different kind of model to the one that is up there. It is a model, well, the capabilities that we now have are quite remarkable, because we are looking at simple things like a three dimensional data-scape as opposed to a two dimensional studio landscape. We are looking at influences and data influences on the city. I mean,

Hani Rashid

Michael Hensel

Singapore is a city where every car driver has a GPS-system, so they know where every taxi is, at any given time and they can actually monitor the traffic and influence it by virtually changing the traffic lights on a computer-operator. So those are things that can be built into a virtual model. And it is an amazing discontent between us, as architects, and urbanists speaking to ourselves internally and what in fact are the needs of the real clients, cities and situations out there. And it is not a stretch for us to start to deploy the findings, the research, the possibilities in much larger and more compelling states and positions. So that is really what I think is part of what we can't fall into, either in this catalogue, or in this show, or these panels, I mean in terms of just going back and talking to ourselves about how wonderful it is to pull in a spline and so on.

PATRIK SCHUMACHER

Can I come in here just to mention something... As you mentioned Singapore, urbanism, huge master plans and splines – that – we did the master plan for Singapore, we won the competition a year ago. And we have completed a master plan that was full of urban design regulations and the first fifteen blocks are already coming out of the ground. It is an unbelievable project that does not have the usual delays but has an unbelievable and serious acceleration. It is important, ... can you hear me?

BART LOOTSMA

Why didn't you show that in this show – out of curiosity?

PATRIK SCHUMACHER

It is in the animations, because the concept of the show is that you have to get into the architecture and then you get glimpses of projects where this conquers a world in larger sets of spaces. And this, just to describe this piece of urbanism which also is not particularly innovative as an aspect of a formal language, but the application, and to convince and win a competition, a real client has these things built, is new. Basically what it is, you have a large open field, you have a series of dispread contacts, different gen(-erated) geometries. You take the software to mediate all these different geometries and use the curvilinear to fuse the different directions to a seamless network of lines. The skyline is just thrown over as a kind of undulated wave and this way you get a kind of continuous field. We know that various different architects will build all these fragments, but a kind of, inverted comma, "smoothing device" of the coherent geometry and the overall coherently deformed and distorted continuously differentiated network, all these notions are very well understood, make sense of this coherency, established domains, regions with open gradient transitions between each other, all this language that we know convinced the client, gave him a totally new sense of urbanism because these other science parts are just kind of individual – the usual concept of space, of establishing a series of containers and dissecting in a series of sub-containers, is taken away and they really got into it and now we are having the problem of having an irritating planning authority on the one hand and economic implementation systems on the other. And now we are working on an implementation strategy of how this model can be maintained, saved and brought forward into a kind of developing process. And I think at that level it is worth noting that we also in a sense of inverted commas, "ripped off" the data-scape idea and concept, and made it real and working, employing a software firm to create a planning tool, where you do all this number crunching and visualizing into a kind of software tool, which the planners are using. So, that is an interesting issue, on the side information, and I am very glad that you are getting involved in this as well.

GREG LYNN

Just so it does not hang out there too long. The inverse proportion between ideologically, socially engaged work and, you know, kind of myopic formalism – I don't think that was ever the case, that these things are inversely related. But I know that the kind of, you know, ironic tragedy of my life is that, more and more, I mean with the Korean church, with the social housing in the Netherlands and now with the WTC competition, I am faced with clients, that are saying "We need something which, you know, has got to work with the victims families groups, it has got to work with the skyline, it has got to work in the media. It has to be totally unprecedented." And so they are saying... well they are not saying: "We want you to do social and ideological work, which is already what we know, you should respond to it, and be an expert on it", they're saying "we need something unprecedented." And that is the social and ideological charge. And it is the same thing with…, I mean, maybe these are kind of the worst case scenarios – of the Bijlmermeer, of the WTC-site, I mean these are all very loaded, heavy, problematic situations. But those situations are looking to advanced formal research to solve these ideological problems. So to say, these things are fighting against each other, you know you are 20% of one and 80% of the other, and in the US we do 80% formal research and 20% ideology, and in Europe it is inverse? I think it is a badly formed argument.

PATRIK SCHUMACHER

There is a misunderstanding. They have to separate these mechanisms to always reconnect, reseparate and reconnect – this oscillation is important. You need time in this oscillation between these two researches, otherwise it establishes a complex barrier, where you scratch your head and walk away. But I do believe, that these are necessary components of a discipline, and it might be stretching our individual careers, usually and theoretically, a work, a formal research, mechanisms and implementation challenges of clients. And you will bring this now to that, but you will not bring that…, you are not solving this in one goal. You either separate into different research groups and different individuals or you separate in career time. They are not opposites, they are necessary complements.

GREG LYNN

The disciplinary work is always already social. Whether it is implemented or not is maybe what you are pointing to, but any kind of work in the discipline has built into it the assumptions about its cultural and ideological force.

PATRIK SCHUMACHER

So, it is quite interesting to hear that you've shifted your position. With respective arguments, that's very interesting, but I… *(Bart Lootsma overlapping in background)*… sorry Bart, I should be watching the screen, I should not be watching my table here…

BART LOOTSMA

Greg, when you say that, I mean previously you were almost kind of profiling yourself as a kind of entrepreneur, right, and then working with a new discipline and you're flown in by people, who need something special. On the other hand you are talking about these social and ethical issues that are somehow embedded in the work. But what are those issues then? Could you formulate that? Could you make that more explicit? Because otherwise it is a kind of simple entrepreneurship, isn't it?

GREG LYNN

Entrepreneurship? That is just the part I do not understand.

BART LOOTSMA

Well, you profile yourself almost as a kind of firm, that offers a certain specialization to people, and people can look you up in the Yellow-pages and ask you to do these things, right? I mean, when you say that in that work all kind of other different agendas are already embedded, what are those agendas, apart from the disciplinary expert?

GREG LYNN

I am not saying that the agendas are there apart from the disciplinary. I'm saying, if you are advancing your disciplinary research, meaning that you are advancing your field, within the terms that the field sets itself up, so in terms of structure, in terms of form, in terms of production, you know, all the way down to myopic little things like putting window openings in a surface, you know, those little innovations have a cultural force and an ideological force, that are already built in. So, the work on variation and differentiation, you know, when you go to a 500-unit-housing renovation, I mean, it is not like I was just interested in variation and all of a sudden thought "Oh!" We have to do a lot of things over and over again, "What a great idea!", you know, built into the system. So we can go through the issues endlessly, but when you look at pushing the field forward, you know within your discipline, the impact of that is already built into the discipline, because the discipline is already embedded, culturally and socially. So, you can't take architecture out of culture and say: "Well, they are doing a thing now, let us put it back and test it". What you do is, you push the field forward, you know in that sense it is inevitable, that it is going to have an impact. But anyway, you know, in terms of entrepreneurship, I don't know, but I had kind

of assumed, that my career would be circumscribed by doing expensive houses and museums and things..., which I've got to say now I am like dying to get a project, which does not involve some kind of tragic problem, you know, but, I would not have thought, I'd be doing social housing. But honestly, I am doing social housing, because that was priorly named in the research I was doing. The problem of variation and iteration is not really so much a museum problem. Museums have different problems, you know, refinement of materials, style, I mean those are bigger problems for museums. I probably will do some social housing before I get to do something like that. But anyway, it was the badly formed question, that got me thinking that was the trajectory I was on.

BART LOOTSMA

But does that mean, that, let's say, the research that you were talking about, the research and the reflection on your discipline, that you do that, not just to work on a discipline with some certain kind of social agendas in the back of your head at the same time?

GREG LYNN

No, I was not being a do-gooder, I was not doing work on variation, because I wanted to do social good. I mean, I am happy to do good – crimes against society and architecture usually spring from trying to do good, you know, much better to be good in the field.

OLIVER SALWAY

I am not sure that this is a direct reaction to what Greg was saying, but I just had one very simple thought, which is that, thank God, we don't agree on anything, all of us, well at least, not too much. I think one thing that was initially quite daunting to me by hearing the title of the exhibition, "Latent Utopias", was thinking, that we were heading somehow towards some idea of one single utopia, that was latent and emerging. And I think, if anything in these times, we see an incredibly great conflict between certainly two distinctive conditions of utopia. But what is comforting about the exhibition title is that little "s" at the end, that makes it plural. We are talking about many different latent utopias. It is either many different latent utopias or it is one latent utopia, that comes in as a divergent degree of plurality, which is fantastic. I think certainly both in terms of form and also urbanism, we face a great pressure from an increasing sense of unity. I can think of one thing, which is a little analogy – there is a bridge, built in London recently, well, it was insufficiently tuned and the problem was, that everybody, walking in the same step, made a huge jump to a point, where it could no longer support itself. And I think that the fact, that it is necessary to break step and keep breaking step, regardless of whether it would be good or whether the ultimate achievement of walking in one direction would be of some great or helpful significance.

BART LOOTSMA

Thank you.

KARI JORMAKKA

Well, if I may interject something. I would actually like to ask Greg, still to come back to the same issue, this variation, this social housing, and so on; do you feel that this is – if you have done formal investigations into the issue of variation, mutation and so on, and then you find an application for this research, in a social housing project, would you say that this is a way of validating the research, that this in some way justifies the research and shows that it was a useful experiment? Is this then, that we find a use, is this a way of justifying the ethic of this original thing? Or is it just incidental that it just happens. And if you say it validates it, would then, for instance, the various uses that we may have for some research, done originally for, let's say the military, that we may find some, well, I don't know what, let's say teflon, who knows what, that we could use in the household, would this then justify research done for the military, for instance? So are you saying that this, when you talk about the discipline, as a whole and the work within the discipline for disciplinary issues such as variation in form, would this later use, as in social housing, this later application, justify this research, justify the discipline?

GREG LYNN

No. I mean, you know, the title of the show is – I mean – latent – you know, what I understand as latent is like latent energy, you know, the bottle has got latent energy, if you provoke it to get it off the table, it's latent energy, its weight will cause it to fall and to crack. So a latent utopia scenario, I think, is – it is the right title for today, because I think to look into the field and say there are latent... – that the research, that has happened, kind of formally and with the introduction of digital technology, that there are latent strategies and techniques, that could be implemented or maybe even are already being implemented, we just are not seeing them or articulating them, I think this is a good matter for, but, you know you could not justify it. You can never justify research. I do not really think, then it is not research.

PATRIK SCHUMACHER

Maybe one could say, retrospectively... maybe not justification, but redemption or validation, because, justification might imply that in the end it had to be justified, otherwise it was unjust and unjustified. The whole point I think is that a certain marginal research has to be validated. Otherwise this whole branch of research remains unjustifiable. But the whole 100%, I would argue, of a branch of research is redeemed, if a certain percentage starts to take root and makes a vital contribution to the development of civilisation, if you like, and helps to establish another level of evolutionary stage or achievement. That is extremely important and therefore I think, these are precisely the moments, which validate a whole, not only the particular things you have been doing, and you maybe had an intuitive grasp or not, but also validates the tolerance, which was given to you and others, others which might not have been just validated, but have been redeemed, because some of the stuff becomes vitally relevant. I think there was a

similar discovery for us at the AADRL. We said, there is this unbelievable proliferation of an architectural language, of new tools and forms, and it was going on for quite a while, and I felt it was lacking, or it was, the danger seemed to me, that if it goes on for another number of years, it collapses under the weight of, you know talking about potentials too long and nothing coming forward. So I think there is an urgency, we have this oscillation and cycles, where you sieve through and see if these things become vital. For us it was a discovery that a lot of the theoretical terms – concepts of space and concepts of organization, self organization, field, space, etc. was tying in with corporate reorganisational strategies and corporate managerial strategies and systems of business organization. And we tested it through a number of proposals and we got a very, a kind of encouraging feedback, positive feedback from a number of firms, we looked into, we showed the stuff, they were fascinated, whether it was Razorfish, Saatchi&Saatchi, Arup, this particular industry which we picked, from which we knew it could be relevant. I think, it is satisfying to see that someone was coming through and that was NOX and the Soft Office, for instance. So I think, that the awareness of this is very important. But at the same time one of the arguments is we cannot predict it. We cannot straight forwardly aim and craft, and blueprint this. We have to allow these cycles of mutation, recombination, selection and then reproduction. And then reproduction is moved, is given away to let's say other straighter of – maybe no longer the discipline, because the discipline, I think, is that

SPACE CONDITION – INTERNATIONAL ARCHITECTURE SYMPOSIUM

SPACE CONDITION PART 1 PATRIK SCHUMACHER / BART LOOTSMA / MICHAEL HENSEL / KIVI SOTAMAA / GREG LYNN / MARIE THERESE HARNONCOURT 95

evolutionary engine. And then I think, that is the cooperation, this thing, when things become mainstream, which often times is the kind of a moment, when one rejects as part of the discipline. It is the necessary cooperation, the redemption of the discipline.

BART LOOTSMA

Thank you. Michael would like to respond to that.

MICHAEL HENSEL

I actually just have a question, because the word research is used very often at the other table now and I would just really like to know in the plainest terms what you mean by that. Is the research only up to the point of checking different possibilities and limits of technology? Or is research also the part where you take the really articulated piece and you put it into the hand of somebody, so to speak, or let them occupy it in a way? And if you do that, how you do that?

KIVI SOTAMAA

Maybe if I can reply to that. I think there is in Kari's question, that there is a kind of presupposition, a separability between what is a research agenda and a design brief. Michael, your question also indicates, that there is, in the design brief a possibility of feeding back into a system, a kind of ongoing form of research. But the kind of discourse, of which Patrik is talking about, but you are asking in specific terms, the question of research as setting up what it is you do and then whether the fitness of a design brief or if a

particular problem fits that brief. I don't think that is actually the question, because if anything, the most alien of a design brief is able then to reconfigure and put into question what the terms of research are and make it then forced to reassess its performance.

MICHAEL HENSEL

But could you just say what the method of research is, that you employ and how you test things? Because I know that research might have very good impact on the rest of it, on the design brief and the object that is designed, or the rest of it. But I would just like to know by what means you actually conduct ... or anybody who conducts research in the field of design, what does it really imply in kind of laymen's-terms?

GREG LYNN

One is an educator, there is a term I am becoming allergic to, which is "experiment" and there is a term that I am getting interested in, which is "research". And to me, the difference is one of motivation. You know, an experiment tends to be more unmotivated, both within the discipline and in terms of expertise, whereas research is highly motivated and highly expert. And that is, you know, to me, what the next 10 or 20 years is going to be. It is going to be more about research and less about experiments. If that answers...

MARIE THERESE HARNONCOURT

But in the end, the main thing is what comes out of it. Because that you have certain methods to research or develop things, that's clear. Or that you just take some innovations from other professions and everything... I think the main thing is what comes out of it and I think it is interesting in the exhibition, because the whole time there was the word "forms" and I really felt that the word "space" was missing. Because, actually it is an architectural exhibition and I think we are trying to form space. And I think that not just Americans do it, especially in Austria, there has been a great longing for a long time to have a very sculptural way of dealing with space. Maybe in another way, not so much in the generated way, but in a very space forming way. And I think for me the question would be interesting: The form that can become space and architecture and even urban strategy, I say, – a very big span – but I believe in this: if you started off with an architecture which has content, then the form has the content and also the system or the structural thinking for the city, for the house – it's not a matter of measurement I think. It could be used, it could be worked out in each

measurement, if you have these parameters and I was interested in this discussion, with all these critics sitting there, what kind of potential they think, the formal or spatial formal studies could have, also for future concepts, for programmatic concepts, because I think, that there is a lack of spatial awareness and it could be a possibility and we see it with all the research that is done, and I think it's so important, how can you bring these forms into architecture, into space and I know that a lot of very nice studies of form don't yet manage, to get into space and I think, this is also a big thing that we have to work on and the research is important and also what the next step could be.

Continued on page 113

Interviews 3

kabru
propeller z

Heywon Seo

Welcome, kabru of propeller z! My first question is: how would you characterise your work in general?

kabru

If you look at it superficially, our work appears extremely formal. However, this form is the result of a search that is based on a concept. This concept is the most essential part of our work and always deals with the question of what would be the best result for

the client, even if they might see things differently at the beginning. The form then results from the three-dimensional development of the concept.

Heywon Seo

I would like to quote Christian Muhr: "The future of the arts might be multi-media and possibly architecture will never experience this future, but dissolve in the synthesis of multiple media". How would you perceive the role of the architect in the future?

kabru

Christian Muhr's texts are always rather cynical and outré – which is why we like working with him – however, of course the influence of the media cannot be denied. The media is getting stronger and stronger, which can mainly be observed in styling – and in this symposium, too, the main focus of the discussion is on styling and form and not so much on space. Still, architects will always do what they were commissioned to do, for as long as man does not dissolve into cyberspace and end up walking around as a cyborg in virtual space. This means that they will continue to create spaces for people in order to protect them from the environment.

The influence of the media and their connections with architecture will, of course, continue to increase. For us this is also a very interesting field, an atmosphere of departure triggered by the media and with which we want to try to keep pace.

Heywon Seo

What were the practical consequences of the use of computers for your work?

kabru

Of course, things are a lot different now than they were before. We often worked with drawing sheets, sheets as big as the tables on which we now can produce our drawings with the computer. We were not able to imagine planning a virtual space and I was always scared that I would lose the overview of the room. Now, I sit down in front of the machine, switch on the screen and an endless virtual space opens up before me and I can start to build my ideas in it. Especially in the field of 3D visualisation, the computer has meanwhile become a very important medium, as a volume operation delivers results much faster and more easily than building models, thereby changing the process of developing shapes considerably. We are trying to master the 3D program, which is of course difficult. On the other hand, I have noticed that the work of many of my colleagues is mastered or even dominated by the 3D program itself, and we try to work against that.

Heywon Seo

There are five of you in the office – to what extent is it really possible for five people to supervise a project on the scale of "Meteorit", for instance? Do you carry out implementation planning, detail planning, construction supervision and so on yourselves? How can you guarantee that an idea is really implemented in this way?

kabru

Of course we prefer to accompany a project from

beginning to end, including the call for tender, detail planning, cost estimate, construction supervision and handing over, because architecture usually tends to change on the construction site. Our kind of architecture in particular, and also the work of many of my younger colleagues, is very detailed. This is why it is particularly important to check the details on site. If you don't, the result becomes a mere copy of the first, original design concept. We often use material in which mistakes cannot be resolved as easily as, say, with plasterboard, so we have to include every single little screw in our plans.

Heywon Seo

Do you have a message for today's students?

kabru

This is difficult for me, as I am myself still a student, so this message goes to myself as well. The only thing I would like to say is that students, despite tuition fees, which will hopefully soon be abolished, should take their time with their studies. This period is a buffer, a kind of reservoir for a professional life during which one has very little time usually to focus on one area and carry out detailed research. So, better to study for a couple more years now than to look back and regret not having taken the time afterwards!

Chris Bagot, Oliver Salway

Softroom

Anja Jonkhans

If I may start with the first question, which is quite a general one: How would you characterize your work and how would you describe your specific kind of architecture?

Oliver Salway

We always wanted to produce work that is both: theoretical, abstract and conceptual but also practical, commercially successful and accessible to as many people as possible.

Chris Bagot

We also like to look to the future. We strive toward some simple ideals like quality and beauty. We want to stimulate people, to make them think and to make them enjoy the work just quite directly. So, a lot of that comes from an instinctive approach of what we think will trigger emotions of people.

Anja Jonkhans

What would be the project which would describe your ambitions in that case?

Oliver Salway

Well, the easiest thing is to look at the projects that have perhaps been most popular in the sense that they have been requested for republication over and over again. There was one project in particular – now it's quite a long time ago – which we did for the "Wallpaper"-magazine. They'd asked us to come up with the design for a flexible apartment and we responded by taking the metaphor of a Swiss-Army-knife, blowing it up to this big kind of eight meter long object. I think that that is quite a good example of what we mean of doing a project that is conceptual. Of course, you could take the same idea and do a very abstract piece of work with it but we wanted to illustrate those ideas about flexibility and control and how you utilize space in a very engaging and direct way. Something, that you can flip through in a magazine, competing with the cookery and the fashion section but you come across that piece of conceptual architecture, which is kind of immediate and fun and almost pop-y but still has a thinking behind it.

Anja Jonkhans

What is your personal cultural background and how does it influence your work?

Chris Bagot

We both studied at the Bartlett School of Architecture in London and I think we were quite lucky with our timing. We started studying architecture at a very interesting time, when the school was changing and going from a quite conservative institution which taught architecture in isolation, to suddenly inviting all these people from all over Europe. It changed from being an English school of architecture to being an international one.

So it became this fantastic hive of ideas and I think that was crucial to our development. We had our eyes opened to the potential

that architecture can engage with all sorts of other kinds of media and different creative ideas. And being in London – being surrounded by fashion and music and everything else – I think I never want to be anywhere else.

Oliver Salway

I think that this is true but also we were young enough and arrogant enough, as you are when you are a young student and you think that everyone is talking rubbish, that we were prepared to look beyond it. The new people were not god-like figures – they were just these new tutors that had arrived. Some of them were very academic, very theoretical and impractical in their methodology and their approach but it was good for us to have that and it was also a very good background for us to react against.

Anja Jonkhans

Where did you grow up and how did this influence your work?

Oliver Salway

I grew up splitting time between being in the countryside and being in Birmingham, which was developed in the Victorian era. So it's a dark and imposing town that has also massive post-war constructions which is very modern as well, but quite bleak in a sense. So I have that on the one side and on the other side I had a kind of blissful countryside with little

sheep and cows and old stone buildings. My father was very involved in the University at Oxford and so I also have this whole cultural background. It was really kind of a clash between the two – but at the age of eighteen I went to London and I never went back.

Chris Bagot

I grew up in a place which is about one hour south of London which means, that everyone would look away from the place we were in towards London. So I was just happy to escape as soon as I could and it was London, where my cultural and architectural thinking really began.

Anja Jonkhans

There is a huge discussion running across Austria, what the

role of an architect is supposed to be. One faction says it is more the designer, the artist with the huge utopian ideas, the other side believes in managing and controlling. What do you think will be or already is the role of an architect?

Chris Bagot

If you look around the world, you can see that architects should spend more time doing the design part and my worry is that there aren't enough architects who have the skill to do that. I also don't have a problem with the idea that some of the processes can be managed by other people. You just have to make sure, that the process is managed by people who are not just sympathetic to architects and architecture but who actively want to support the role of the architect as a designer of cities and spaces.

Oliver Salway

I would broadly agree with that. I think, that architects always find themselves in a difficult position because people attribute everything about a work of architecture to the individual part of the architect, which is very much not the case. I think that the team needs to be acknowledged a bit more.

It is one classic thing about architects: you want to take credit for everything but you shouldn't and people want you to take credit for everything but probably you shouldn't either. So I think, a sort of more common recognition of the reality of the process would be very helpful.

Anja Jonkhans

Now, how long do you actually follow your projects or how long do you guide them in the sense of detailing?

Chris Bagot

All of our projects we have seen all the way through to completion and we have probably done a lot of drawings which is why we don't make as many projects as other architects. And we've also chosen very good construction-people to work with us. So the development of the detail-design is done in collaboration with the people who are building.

Oliver Salway

The British contractual system works with architecture in the way, that the architect makes a design and then the contractor deals directly with the client to produce this piece of work. The architect continually monitors the building process, that's how it has been traditionally, so the architect has an input all the way along to the end.

But for about 15 years there has been an increasing rise of what is called "design-built", where the contractor takes the main responsibility initially with the client and the architect is really only a consultant in the process and his involvement stops at a certain point. That's the way public buildings are done more and more in the UK. We are in our first design-built contract now and there are things that are potentially complicated in this project, so it will be interesting to

see how well they are being realized.

Two buildings have recently been completed by Norman Foster in London. One is a big tower, a very highly crafted building which he built directly for the client. The other building is the City Hall which was done under a design-built contract. And you can see that the quality has suffered to a degree – I mean, it is hard to know exactly what the design was in the first place – but you can see that there has been an extent of degradation in the quality of the one, where the architect was not involved in the whole process.

Anja Jonkhans

You work very strongly with 3D-programms. As far as I know, you started quite early to do so. How far, do you think, have these programmes enabled your projects or your work of architecture?

Chris Bagot

That we've been able to investigate in three dimensions has absolutely been the key to the way we work.

There hasn't been a need to develop ideas through abstracting them into two dimensions as there traditionally has. You can have more ambitious ideas and test them earlier, so you can progress with confidence all the way through the design. You can see much more clearly how the details relate to the whole. I think, that makes the process much more rewarding because it's much more direct. It's more akin to being a sculptor who can deal with a building within his sight, within his grasp throughout the process. I am not saying, that the computer-model is the only way to develop these things but I think, whenever you can work in architecture, to be working in three dimensions is a good thing.

Oliver Salway

That's true and I also think, that there've been a few buildings recently, done by Gehry and Foster and various other people, that could not have been built a few years ago without the computer systems we have.

We haven't produced a work yet, that could not have been produced or built without the computer. All of our projects have not been of that level of technical sophistication but one can very easily see how you could end up at that point.

The other thing is that we also have produced work that has not been built. Whether it is a printed image or a video or whatever – it can only exist because of the computer.

Anja Jonkhans

How important is research and teaching for your work or could it be, if you found the time to do research and teaching in addition to your practical work?

Chris Bagot

We haven't had enough time in the last two years to do research and we don't teach. But one of the reasons why it is necessary, apart from the need to take architecture forward, is that increasingly we are working in a world in which we don't have the time on individual projects to explore ideas as fully as we want

to do. The world is moving too quickly, clients are too demanding and money is to be spent immediately, so you need to have a powerful mechanism for exploring ideas in a more leisurely way. Otherwise you are just going mad because you don't have the time to enjoy your exploration of ideas as it's always been done with time pressure. And that's the main-reason why we want to do more research.

Oliver Salway

I think you aren't only going mad but also the work gets increasingly diluted because you are expected to put down a kind of immediate reaction all the time. We've been working on one project over the last year, that has had incredibly tight deadlines week after week after week. But at the beginning of that project there was a period of a month or two, where the client essentially paid us just to do research. And had we not done that, it would have been quite impossible to do the project. It was an incredibly luxurious process and something that would be really very nice to repeat but we are not expecting any other clients to be so indulgent with us. So the responsibility is for us now to set up programmes within our own studio to have ongoing research and I would agree that it's absolutely the key – definitely.

Anja Jonkhans

First I would like to ask you, how would you characterize your work and your buildings?

Stuart Veech

Before we started our work in Austria (first we were based in London) we looked at the upcoming digital revolution of the late eighties and the beginning nineties and how that would influence architecture.

We set up our office in Vienna in 1992 basically with the idea of fusing media and architecture together – media as architecture and architecture as a medium. So we've done a series of projects in the last ten years of television and film, installations and different events,

exhibitions and mobile architecture and also virtual architecture. The main issue for us is the idea of fusing virtual and real architecture, so that the borders and boundaries blur.

Anja Jonkhans

How does your cultural background influence your work and your working attitude and what do you think is the role of an architect?

Mascha Veech-Kosmatschof:

Stuart is from Chicago, I was born in Moscow. I studied at the "Angewandte Kunst" in Vienna and Stuart at the AA in London. Everybody asks us why we actually

settled in Vienna and I say well, Vienna does give us a lot of different possibilities. Stuart started to work on the re-design of the corporate identity at the ORF at the time of Neville Brody, that was actually the start. But later on it developed into something completely different, to this more broad type of office, interdisciplinary office which is constantly switching between art, design and architectural themes. I think, it gives us a great freedom and a more global view of things, that our roots are actually not in Austria. We are between our home bases where we are from and we can overlook lots of things and just select the most positive aspects of Vienna, for example, where we are situated.

Concerning the role of the architect: the main role of our office is experiment and research. Research of possibilities of the new materials, of translating the digitally generated forms into real environment or real architecture. We are constantly switching between reality and virtual reality, trying to find ways of merging them, and to find the right material for that because we can do all this computer-generated new architecture which is upcoming or already started ten years ago, but the material-industry is not that far. They don't give us the proper materials for realizing all these organic forms. So we are working very closely with them, trying to

Mascha Veech-Kosmatschof, Stuart Veech

veech.media.architecture

motivate them and to get them involved in research. We see our role on the verge of the nano-technology. This is the biggest utopia we can think of right now and it is a broad field of new materials, which the technologies are going to give us.

Stuart Veech

I think there are two types of utopia: there was a utopia back in the eighties, that was also coming out in the nineteen sixties, about communication, revolution, information, the idea of the internet and that's going to change everything. We were in London at the time, looking at this issue and we said: great, that sounds wonderful, that seems to be very interesting, but nobody really knew what was going to happen. Now we are in this phase where everything becomes computer-generated but nobody knows how to realize these things. Everything is kind of morphed, kind of blobby, kind of mutated, but the materials are still the same: steel, glass, wood, concrete and nobody is thinking how

to translate this. What is a transparent architecture, what is a translucent architecture, if you use normal glass panels? That's not going to be the same. There are a lot of things in the exhibition which are not standard architectural forms and right now there is no way to produce these things.

In our office we have to address the issue of how to produce certain objects in certain environments and we have to be very creative about how to use materials which you can have at hand, creating a completely new effect.

With nano-technology it is completely different. When you have glass-panels for example, which are not normal glass-panels, you could have translucent materials, which are as strong as steel. But I think, architects don't even look at these things. They don't look at the technologies.

For them, the software is the computer and the computer is the technology and they don't think about the production of the objects.

But architecture is not something that is just on a screen. Architecture should be an idea that is being realized and right now we are in the phase where things are basically stuck on the screen, a kind of suspended animation. Maybe some of these things will be built at some point. But that's the question, whether they will be satisfying to the architects or satisfying to the client or to the people who are living in the cities where these things are going to be constructed.

Anja Jonkhans

But research is very time-consuming and cost-consuming as well. So, where does it actually take place? Does it take place while teaching at university or while working on the projects in your office, together with the industry?

Stuart Veech

Well, basically architects are trained to work 24 hours a day. They have a vision and it doesn't go away. It's not a profession where they just turn off after nine to five and that's

it. Architects always look that exhausted because they have a dream and it's a question of realizing this dream. This takes research, it takes a lot of politics and motivating people, be it the producers or the clients, to realize the dream. Researching takes place with producers. When you talk to clients about experiments or doing research they get worried about it. When we talk with the producers about it, we argue about these issues, about how far we can go. Mascha takes the more radical side and says: we have to go further. I look at the side and I say, well, I have to convince these people in order to produce it, and then we switch roles.

Teaching gives you another view of the kind of problems which you deal with every day. It gives you the chance to go into another phase, where you can deal with crazy projects and crazy ideas but at the same time you are looking at these ideas the students throw out on the table and sometimes you think well, that's really interesting, how could you realize that. I think it becomes very helpful in a kind of sense to free yourself from all the problems we have – and we produce problems very fast – so it is nice to take at least a couple of hours a week off and think about other problems.

Anja Jonkhans

But if you are very keen to bring projects to their limits, then how far can you actually overlook the project? Are you detailing yourself or do you give it away to someone else?

Stuart Veech

Our office is simply doing a lot of testing and we have very short-term projects. The client says: look, we have six weeks, we want something incredible, we want some image-project, we want something which is fantastic, there it is. Take it or leave it. And we say ok, we'll take it. And then we are developing the project till the last minute. We aren't bored, we are sweating it out with the producers, having a belief and an idea that it's going to work, but not really knowing how it's going to work.

Mascha Veech-Kosmatschof

We know how it works!

Stuart Veech

Yes, we know how it works, it's a calculated risk. A lot of stuff is not done through drawings, but from testing the materials and making different samples of how the things are working. And through the samples you get a feeling of how it's going to be and of course you get to a certain point when you say, ok let's produce it.

Mascha Veech-Kosmatschof

But of course we don't let anything out of our hands – it's the biggest mistake architects actually could make in our eyes, to give up control of a project after a certain phase.

Stuart Veech

But that's forced by the economic situation, where clients actually want to take it away from architects and give it to somebody who is controlling the project. And if the architects who are the creative force behind the project are taken out, then you can forget about the architecture. I think our results would never be what they are if we didn't take it all over for ourselves.

Anja Jonkhans

Is there a project about which you would say you have worked most successfully all the way through, in the way you wanted to imply your thoughts and your ideas in that concept?

Stuart Veech

For me it's hard to take out one project. But to talk about "Zeit im Bild" – this was a project, where we had to be on board the whole time. It is actually interesting, because it is one of the largest projects, we ever had, and it worked quite well.

We also had projects like the Kunsthalle-exhibition, in Vienna which was a killer-project. There were so many dangerous points in the project but you get over these troubles and every project has the same problems, in a way.

End of Interviews 3

Space condition part 1 continued from page 96

CHRISTOPH PICHLER

Marie Therese, Marie Therese, this is Christoph from downstairs. I'm absolutely with you, I think this is one of the best statements of the whole conference, because we are talking about forms here, we are talking about formalisms, we are talking about objects and we are not talking about space. We are talking about representation of interaction and we are not talking about actual interaction. So we are talking about the virtual and not about the real. And I think it would have been a good idea to have had the conference after the exhibition opening or even better within the exhibition or in front of the objects everybody is exhibiting, because then you could refer the words to our work and I think, the conference is, in a way, a blob, which is hovering somewhere and not in a way routed or grounded to the work we do and I think it would be very interesting to see our words confronted with the work we do and it would be interesting for the audience as well.

MARIE THERESE HARNONCOURT

I have to make a quick answer, because I think I was a bit misunderstood, because I believe in the virtual and I don't think that everything has to be just in this realisation, realistic state. I think it's important to dream and to think about this not having everything down to earth – just so that there is no misunderstanding of my statement.

KARI JORMAKKA

The next discussion will take place in 10 minutes. Again we have two blocks, one with Aaron Betsky as moderator, Nigel Coates, propeller z, MVRDV, the other with Xavier Costa moderating, agps architects, Sadar Vuga architects, UN Studio, veech.media.architecture and Ross Lovegrove.

Space Condition Part 2

Aaron Betsky with
Jacob van Rijs and **Nathalie de Vries**
(MVRDV), **Nigel Coates**
(branson coates architecture),
Philipp Tschofen (propeller z)
in location A

Xavier Costa with
Ben van Berkel (UN Studio), **Ross Lovegrove**,
Nick Bax (The Designers Republic in
collaboration with Sadar Vuga Arhitekti),
Bostjan Vuga (Sadar Vuga Arhitekti),
Reto Pfenninger (agps architecture),
Stuart Veech (veech.media.architecture)
in location B

Due to technical problems with the recording system a brief part of the beginning of the second session is missing.

AARON BETSKY

... and it is to present very powerful images, that then have gone on to live their own lives in public opinion. What is the relationship between the power of the image and its ability to change our perception of reality and the reaction of people who are using or seeing the building on a daily basis. How does it integrate or refuse to integrate itself into daily life?

JACOB VAN RIJS

Yes, it is quite remarkable, almost shocking I think, that architecture still, that there is a debate and that there is a totally different debate in society and then people who have a certain wide opinion about things can have a very narrow minded opinion about architecture. And this is somehow what we focus on and never what we feel. And when a project is realized and completely harmless, and gets such an enormous violent reaction from others, that's a question you can ask yourself – why does that happen? And I have the feeling that has to do with what is still a very conservative view on architecture from the general public.

AARON BETSKY

Are you making utopian buildings?

JACOB VAN RIJS

Yeah, sometimes, mostly, I hope so.

XAVIER COSTA

OK, let's continue. I wanted, before presenting the people at our table participating in the discussion, I wanted to make a comment about the previous discussion this morning and about some of the main topics that have been posed. Since we were starting with the concept of utopia and asking ourselves "what is the role of utopia and nowadays for architects?" I also wanted to make a reference to a wider context. When we look at modernism, utopian modernism was an objective for architects, but also for artists as well. And the project of architecture and art at that point was inseparable in this horizon of utopia. When we ask ourselves about how utopia maintains its position in the architectural discourse nowadays, I think it is also useful to have a view of what artists are doing and how this very concept of utopia is present in our practice nowadays. Since we were also discussing this pair of concepts, discipline versus context, Greg Lynn was addressing this issue earlier on. When we look at the work of artists nowadays and the way this work is also being presented, we have had recent important manifestations like Documenta or even like the Venice Biennale, we realize that artists then increasingly do work in an area that some of them have described as the editing of reality. That means the artist is willing to leave behind the possibility of an artistic discipline and to immerse herself or himself into, let's say the thick reality of social issues, of production, of technology, of politics and to produce that, I think this is a good description, this editing of reality, to transform reality and at the same time to cast a meaning, to cast a significance on this. This seems to be an issue that is relevant also for architects and this came up earlier on. How the architect can also influence this reality with his or her production. And also at the same time how capable is this architect of redefining this reality in the way contemporary art is managing to do. Well, we have with us, to introduce quickly the participants at this table, we have with us Ben van Berkel, starting from my right. I am not going to introduce them; just quickly present their names, Mascha Veech-Kosmatschof and Stuart Veech, Reto Pfenninger, Ross Lovegrove, Jurij Sadar and Bostjan Vuga and finally Nick Bax from the Designer's Republic. I would like to hand over the microphone to Ben van Berkel and pick up on what Nathalie and Jacob were discussing.

AARON BETSKY

Xavier, can I ask Ben? I cannot hear what Ben is saying. But I would love for Ben to say what he, because he has spoken a great deal about the need to make highly recognizable buildings that act kind of like focal points within an environment, and I would like to ask him how he feels about the possibilities for misinterpretation and whether he believes that his objects are a kind of harbinger, a sort of promise for utopia. I think this is something that Ben should and could be able to answer.

BEN VAN BERKEL

Thank you Aaron. So, I just stepped in, I did not exactly follow what you were discussing, when I stepped in. This is a concrete question. Well, maybe you know, we in our work we have been exploring all possibilities of utopia of the maybe

last 5, 6 years. Not so much related to the effect of the final concrete aspect of the work itself, but also specifically related to contemporary techniques. I, for a long time, thought that we misinterpreted our own possibilities to explore the profession from the inside out. So questions of geometry and material research, problematic and infrastructural, may be combinations, to explore it not only by means of the computer, but to rethink our techniques. Like maybe we have seen in the profession before, by someone who discovered and developed his own techniques like someone like Borromini who knew through particular drawings, stereometric axos, you could call them, to explore the possibility of extruding the dome. We believed, that we could rethink spatial, organizational aspects of what we make through contemporary techniques in order to look beyond the reality of everyday. Because my belief was that, actually for a long time, specifically around the 70ies and 80ies and the early 90ies, a lot of architects were working with the notion of the linguistic, the metaphorical, with the representational. Whereas I thought that, and actually I am not the only one, there is a group of architects who opposed this strategy of working, that we needed to work with the actual aspects of architecture itself. So instead of being representational we wanted to work with the actual elements of architecture, on what could be explored. So to be more instrumental instead of being representational. And the critique was more or less that maybe we believed that architecture became very one-dimensional. Often architecture was only one statement or was to be made to amuse, or was to be made to quote historical references. And I thought, that was really hollowing out the profession, when we were particularly exploring these contemporary techniques. Anyway, that is not an answer to your question. I am talking too much about the intro of the answer. My answer to, let's say, the way, how let's say, through new technics, in the way you can then explore new spatial and organizational principles in any way, I believe, especially through the earlier comment made about art, architects today should rethink, in a way, how their work could be misinterpreted and be reinterpreted. And how their work could generate something that could not be explained, and at the same time could generate a lot of different names of what you have not been calculating for the project. So in that sense I do believe that in..., for that reason, the interpretation we heard before, is quite interesting. Artists in my opinion, often – a good artist and good art – often draw the viewer, the public back to the piece itself more often.

So you remember it, you like to recall the piece if it is good. So, yes, I believe, that what you make through contemporary technologies with an option of going beyond reality and looking into the future, and giving maybe the work more than only the pure techniques which I talked about before, but to maybe rethink it through the way you can work with artists for instance. You could give architecture far more layers, than maybe we have seen in the last maybe 10, 15 years. We should rethink in that position how we work as architects and I don't know if that is an answer or maybe a further question for the rest of you on the other side. But what then is the role of the architect? I do believe that in that sense architects should totally rethink their position as being the singular, classical designer, making one building. I have said that now for the last three years, that I believe that architects should be more public scientists, and collect, rework and rethink their position and change their practice.

XAVIER COSTA

I would also like to make a comment about Aaron's question. I think it's a very relevant one. If I understand properly what you were addressing, it is about the reception of architecture and to what extent it is the architect's task or what are the strategies of control over this reception.

AARON BETSKY

Yes Ben, I think it is interesting, what you said and I was hoping it could be more specific about somebody's buildings as I hope all the architects can be, but an essence of one of his arguments is, that the work of architecture, especially when it has the kind of utopian tendencies that we see in this show, functions as an artwork and that's why it has the right to be, to put it very simply, different. And that if it is good, it is good because it brings in so many interpretations and it persists in memory long enough that it performs the way an art-object does, in a culture, which, you say, it doesn't perform, it's not useful, but it actually has the task of altering uses of perceptions around it. That's a pretty coherent argument, but I think I would take as a lead, maybe turn to either propeller z or maybe Nigel Coates, because it seems that Nigel has taken, in some ways, a radically different approach which is one of kind of scanning and reinterpreting the images that are already out there and trying to use those to dissolve the traditional object of architecture, but maybe I got it wrong?

NIGEL COATES

I would say, that we – as a practice-approach – see architecture from the outside-in, so the opposite of Ben, and that is to use the city, lives in cities, people and the body, as a way of creating agendas for architecture, that has to do both with the object, perhaps, but also to the way that architecture interfaces with new architecture, it can interface with the present one that we have. And one of the aspects of the show that I find odd from my personal point of view, is the apparent lack of images of people, or people moving, or any hint of the sensual dimension, the almost film-made dimension of everyday life. So, what might this mean in terms of practising as an architect? I think, that it's important as an architect, to kind of have many different positions within the spectrum of what it means to practise. Namely that if you are actually designing a building that's going to be constructed, you approach that with a certain mentality. But if you are pursuing a more research and theoretical dimension of architecture, of course you must go further. But what really interests me is the point at which that further imagining dreaming can come back and reconnect to the world that we live in. And a concrete example of that might be Diller and Scofidio's cloud in Switzerland, which I happened to go to rather late in the day last weekend. And it succeeds in being iconic, you recognize it immediately, having once understood it

or seen it. Even more so, if you've been inside it. What I like so much about it is that there is a physical structure, which is almost industrial in nature and it produces this mist, and the mist is completely subject to the wind and pressure conditions of the air around it. But to actually go there is so much better, I think, than seeing it in a picture or even in a film and the reason is, that the mist can drift between the other exhibits that form that particular campus of pavilions around that end of lake Neuchatel and it seems to capture the public imagination. People were absolutely loving being in it, they loved the experience, they loved putting on plastic-macs, they loved the fact, they were in a rainy space, they loved the fact that the whole thing had a simultaneous artificial and a natural quality. And I suppose, that in our more extreme thinking, that we imagine something like that, that rather than imagining, rather rigid but beautifully fluid digital forms, that kind of sit on a white screen, we try to imagine what it would be like, if there were projections of digital forms in the skies above cities, that could be controlled to move and change shape by the citizens, using their mobile phones to activate and make them progress.

AARON BETSKY

Xavier, it might be interesting to hear from Ross Lovegrove in relationship to that.

ROSS LOVEGROVE

I just actually came straight in from Hollywood, where I just had remarkable discussions with some very important directors out there, who wrote me a letter and said that my designs point toward the future, which is a very hard thing to live up to. But anyway, I wanted to talk with them about how my work would integrate into the area of film and they contacted me mainly about a production that is set in the year 2069. And it was quite remarkable to go to the Fox-set and to see how in an instant making kind of whip up architecture or trains or anything, that comes to mind within the time-frame of something like a week. But in speaking to the production designers out there, it was very evident, that these people live and work in a microcosm, the microcosm of Hollywood and how disconnected they are from these ideas, such as the mist that Nigel was talking about, which I've seen, which I found quite magical myself, because of work near there or a client there. But in trying to describe to these people a vision of the future I can't help but think about Tokyo, still, 'cause I was just there, before being in the States, and this energy, that surrounds people in a city like Tokyo, which obviously doesn't surround people in a place like London or here in Graz, that kind of energy-level that exists, with the colour and the vibrancy that's brought there, I find very exciting, although, in a sense, you know I've been asked to talk about this now, and I've sat through the debates this morning and I felt actually more comfortable in those debates this morning, with the themes and there were one or two moments where I thought I could have talked and then, here I am thrust in the middle of 500 architects and I am the only non-architect, I presume, here, and that can be quite unnerving. The reason I'm here is the invitation, of course, but I mean: I look at this whole debate on architecture

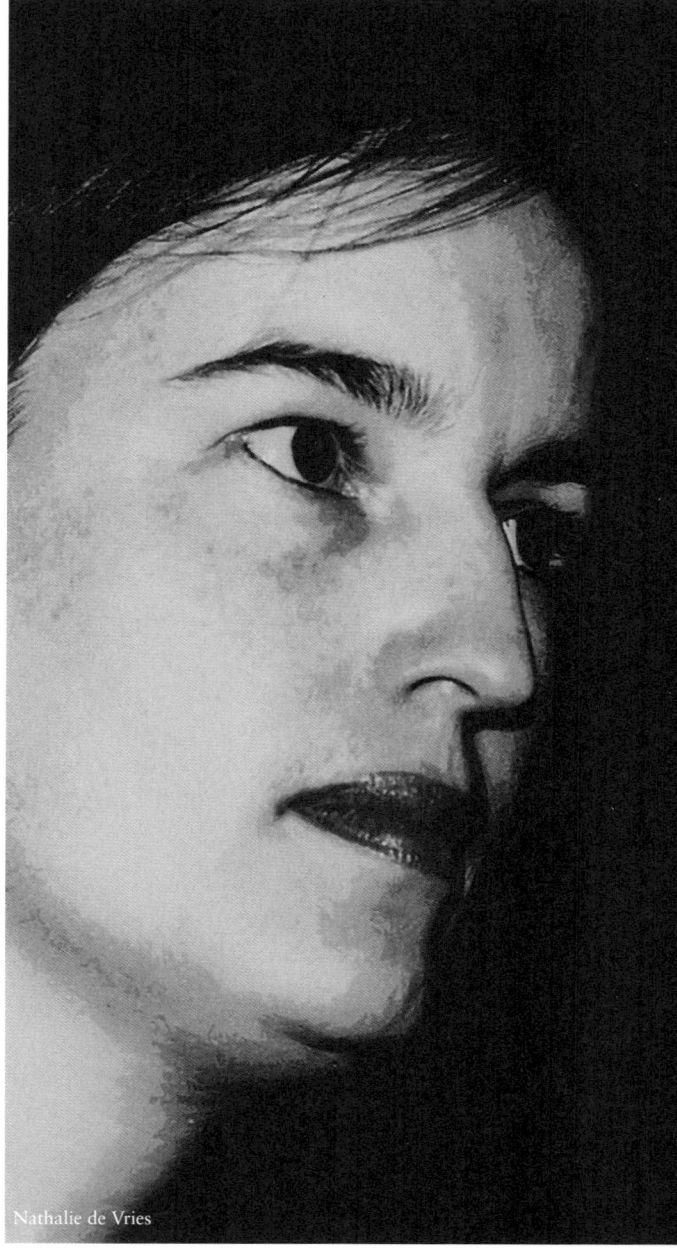

Nathalie de Vries

Ross Lovegrove

a different way and I think that if you relate visions of Tokyo, visions of Hollywood through the eyes of a product designer, or not even a product designer, I am somebody who works currently between the worlds of automotive design and aircraft interiors. I've just been asked to do a building in Tokyo and Shibuya, I worked with Issey Miyake, I worked across the board between fashion, architecture products, right across the board, and I'm constantly somebody, who is like a bee, that floats buzzing, I pollinate industries and it's that pollination of industries, which gives rise to very new ways of thinking and potentially a new physicality and I'm often disappointed, when I enter into fields, at how isolated those fields are. I don't necessarily feel that about architecture, right now – having gone to the Biennale in Venice I was totally blown away by the Arsenale and I felt an amazing presence and energy of new materials, physicality, structures, a sort of global consciousness, that there is this new way forward, and even if you challenge the logic, which you can on many points, there is this willingness in people now, to want to build form, and I find that very primordial and therefore very instinctive and very right. So within my own work, which as I enter more and more into perhaps the field of the built environment where I can put my small object, my medium size object and so on, into that and form a holistic relationship, I see a path opening up of two directions: I see one of how to deal with the new physicality because you can only do that through understanding manufacture and manufacture normally only gives you symmetry, it doesn't give you asymmetry at all, and it doesn't give you transparency very easily at the cost. That challenge is pretty much, most, what I see. And on the other hand I see a direction emerging – you've got a very polished future emerging in the utopian sense – of precision and versatile manufacturing, on the other hand, you have, what I call, "craft-tech", which is more about carbon fibrous, non-coloured, non-glossy structures. They will come 'cause all the discussions which I have with people around the world, like Adriaan Berghuis from Delft and so on, about how to build structures, or people like Cecil Balmond, these kinds of people – absolutely fantastic – so you are seeing a convergence, I think, between all worlds, right now, and I hope, there is enough spirit to allow influences all ways and if any of you have time and go to visit the Anish Kapoor installation at the Tate, it will blow you away, I mean that's a piece of architecture like I haven't seen in years – it's absolutely remarkable.

XAVIER COSTA

I don't know if you would like to respond to this, or... – it seems Ross was making this point about his view from a territory, which is partly in architecture but also in other fields and since we also have here The Designers Republic, I wonder if you would like to maybe continue on this comment.

NICK BAX

Well, what I wanted to say, as a non-architect also... – you know, The Designers Republic, we are not architects, but we do work with architects, such as Sadar Vuga, on a piece, an installation for the "Latent Utopias" exhibit. I just thought, I wonder how architects feel about working with designers.

Not like on a cosmetic sort of level at the end of a project, but actually at the very start, a concept of an idea, and working with them on the genesis of an idea and not just a later level where it is just applying graphics to polish the overall building or whatever the project is. And I just wonder what their feelings are about working with designers at this sort of concept, this sort of level. And the discussion, as it was earlier about, what is an architect, what does architecture involve?, and we are looking at your professions and what you actually do, and just how you feel about working with designers at that sort of level? I just wonder, what the rest of the panel and everyone here thinks about it.

AARON BETSKY

There seems to be a notion emerging, that what makes the work under discussion, in absence of the exhibition, utopia is somehow, that it is art, and if we could only be an Anish Kapoor, then we'd really be in great shape, but maybe that is better than Kapoor because it is more complex. I mean, the discussion seems to be – several times it has moved around this notion, that perhaps what it is, that architecture does, that is worthy of it being put in an exhibition like that, is that it works in a way that in our culture we usually call art, that is why it is interesting about Kapoor and things like that but so it is either art for future or something else.

NATHALIE DE VRIES

My first answer was rather avoiding that question, I must admit. But I guess I have to say that, and it also concerns the project we sent in for the exhibition, that 90% of the time the people who commission us, and the people who are going to use the buildings that we are making, and the urban designs that we are making, approach us with the question: "We know what it is like, now, but we also know that we somehow feel not very comfortable with the idea, that we have to be in such a type of building, or live in such a building in the future. Help us to think of another way to deal with this type of program." I come from a country where we talk a lot with the future client, with the people who are going to use it, with the people who live in the direct neighbourhood, with colleagues and it's all, well, it is not very mysterious, how projects develop, because this happens in cycles, every phase of the project, everything is debated over and over again. So, what I'd like to say actually is that none of our projects could have existed in the way they do without actually a big influence from the clients and people who are now using these buildings. And even afterwards we are often asked to come along and we have e-mail contact with inhabitants of buildings. What I'd like to say is, we should not underestimate the urge of people themselves to change their environments, to make things different or better, and often the critiques of the projects are quite superficial, they often deal with very visual aspects and indeed images of the buildings, that are sent out through the press. I even noticed sometimes that quite innocent details of the building become the major part of discussion about a building, for example, as in an office building, we made the ramp, which is actually decorative in some ways, becomes the

major focal point. What I would like to say is, yes, we do want to make buildings for the future, as well, but also because we are asked to do so by clients and often architects don't know everything about everything, so often the people who are coming with the projects, bring up their own utopian ideas into the projects.

AARON BETSKY

That is an interesting issue that comes up there, because one of the other implications of the exhibition but I think of – also especially of MVRDV's work – is that there is a set of negotiations, calculations, of prognostication, of research phase, that transforms itself through an internal logic into something, that has a built form, but a built form is only one particular phase in the project and either the building keeps changing as in some of the flowing buildings, or because of the way it is used and perceived, the project continues. And in the Netherlands, where I now live, they are obsessed with the notion of project-based working. But this has an interesting analogy to some of the generative programs that some of the computer based people use. Maybe, Xavier, we can throw it back to you and hear from our friends from Ljubljana, how they see themselves in that context.

XAVIER COSTA

The topic that is opening up is the issue of collaboration between disciplines or interdisciplinary work between architects, we've talked about designers, we could also refer to the role of media in these collaborations. So, both, Ben van Berkel and Ross also opend up this issue of interdisciplinary work. But since you were also collaborating with Nick, would you like to react to this?

BOSTJAN VUGA

Yes, I mean, I would say I strongly agree with what Nick said before. Particularly because we work together in a kind of inter-group, a sort of way of working meaning that we develop concepts together. It is not like plastic surgery or make-up, which is added at the end, it is actually real collaboration from the very beginning. And basically a kind of spanning of the border of architecture as a discipline and graphic design as a discipline. It is the main aim. But at the end of the day the effect we want to achieve is actually to generate a new experience. This is basically the point, I'm trying to refer to what Ben was saying before. It is not a matter of style, it is not a matter of form, kind of structure, not a matter of events. I mean these are all the tools for us and our collaboration, these are all the tools to generate a sort of effect. We generate some new experience. And basically, if I answer the question, Nick stated before, what is actually... – how we see the role of graphic designers: It is actually a very simple thing. We see, you know, that two-dimensional and three-dimensional experience, should be coherent. So basically if you provide something which is 2D and something which is 3D, as a kind of vehicle to generate a new experience, this is actually the aim of our collaboration. And just let me add one thing more: The exhibition there is actually a way, also the book together with it, is actually the way, to show, how we think and work.

Nigel Coates

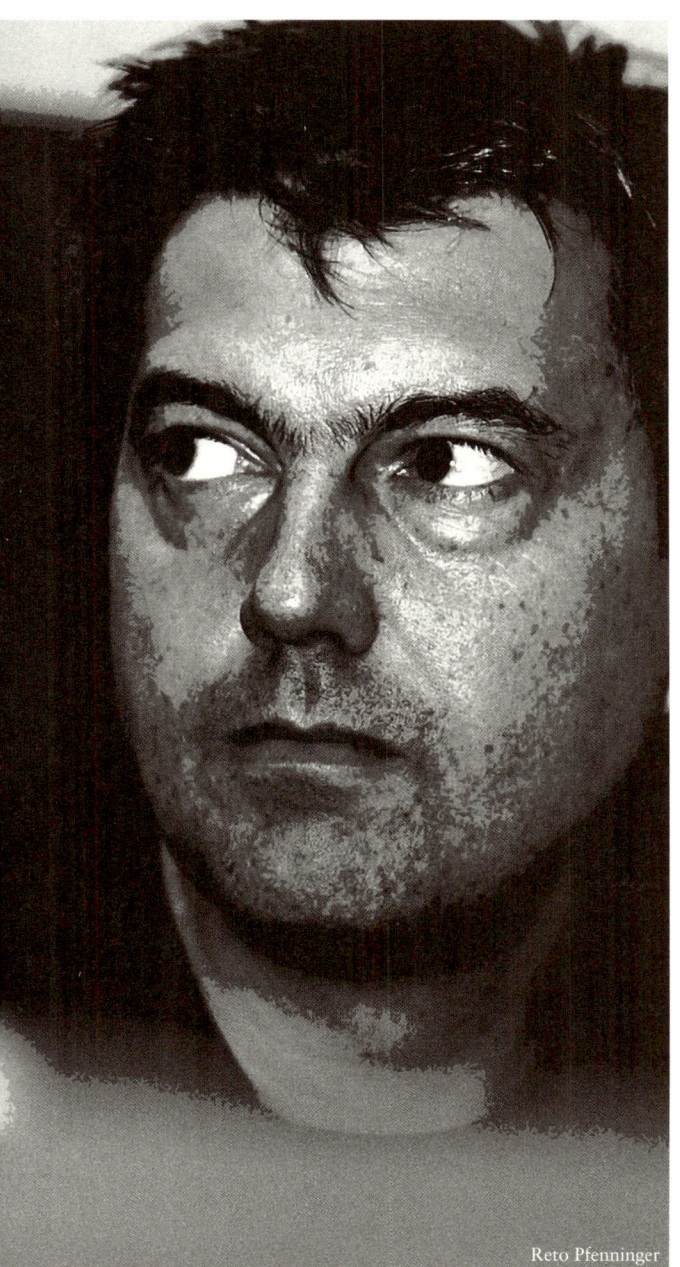
Reto Pfenninger

XAVIER COSTA

Maybe Reto also wants to add something to the issue of interdisciplinary collaboration?

RETO PFENNINGER

It seems to us that more and more the act...

AARON BETSKY

Give him the other microphone!

RETO PFENNINGER

Our starting point is something about the way things evolve and it is, as William Blake, the famous writer, said once, that it is the exuberance of the beauty, that drives us to make architecture that we are always thinking about something about the surplus, something which is a little bit more than we understand at the moment, but we have a kind of an idea about something. And with this team together, all these different people, architecture is going to develop and we do not know where we will arrive. But we hope, that this strong idea is still contained in the architectural objects we make.

AARON BETSKY

We have actually no idea what you said. I think, we should hear from propeller z – whatever, I was just interested, because your work seems not only to exist just at the intersection between the making of buildings and installations and theoretical objects like the tribute to Buckminster Fuller. But also a lot of your realised work is becoming bound up with the world of fashion and display and music and there seems to be a sense that those kinds of environments in that kind of work that architecture does, lends itself to certain utopian tendencies. Perhaps you could comment on that?

PHILIPP TSCHOFEN

It is true that we did some pieces for fashion stores, or for the world of fashion, all of which are luckily not high enough to make it worthwhile to jump from them. I think something that comes across our way of working very often is the topic, that was addressed today a couple of times and that is: could architecture learn or interact with fields like product design, things like an iconic value is something that is extremely important, because products have to be marketed and sold in a very fast cycle. I think that is a very dangerous connection to make. Simply because products can create the wrong context and they have a context in time more than in space, or as architecture has always been the manufacturing of prototypes, so we are always dealing with putting together very many components. And mistakes that are made in a building can not be corrected because the prototype is there and it is what is to be evaluated. I also think, it is a dangerous thing to make the connection between architecture and art, because I think that architecture is there to be evaluated by everybody who uses it and who has to use it. It can not be by-passed, or it can be by-passed sometimes. If you explain architecture as a piece, or the value of a piece of architecture in an artistic context, I think it is a way of avoiding real discussions about the piece. Because, ... why they need to do that is obvious, because of that incredible difference between the design and a built piece. And an

architectural design on paper or even in a model I think, can not be evaluated in all of its ramifications, because nobody would feel threatened by a design, whereas maybe the person who wrote that to the architect, did feel threatened by the built, by the full-scale representation of that design. Because the qualities of the design are manifest in very small things, maybe a little concrete wall that is just on a side of the building, that the architect did not even think about. And this offends that person. So what I want to stress is, that it is extremely important for architecture to be translated into the built world and to be tested there and not to remain and to be re-iterated in a thought or an ideal environment.

AARON BETSKY

That is a good point; I just wanted to be clear that what I was trying to say and I hope, Xavier, that you agree with me, that we don't want just to be generating a discussion, of whether architecture is art. He was merely trying to lay the finger on the notion that the objects, that are worth looking at and that we are seeing on slides and that will be in the exhibition, that is opening tonight, have something about them, that here is called a latent utopia. And I think we have been struggling all day long to try to name, at least some of the qualities, that might encompass, and the obvious sense was, that's got something to do with the future, it's got something to do with design intelligence, it has got something to do with its visual form, its appearance, whether iconic or otherwise, you could have said they are weird, strange, they appear different, they might even be offensive, these are all possibilities and one of the strong possibilities I was offering is that, that aspect of these objects, buildings and interiors, that is not everything they are, but that aspect of them that might make them worth having in an exhibition or which is pointed out by an exhibition, is something that in other contexts is called art and those three letters are a very convenient way of naming something, that is probably too complicated to actually define. But I think Nigel has some rather strong and straightened out opinions about this.

NIGEL COATES

I think it is really important that as an architect, you can use all strategies. But we have this fundamental position that we are dealing with something in the future. As I understand contemporary art at the moment, it tends to deal very much with the moment in which you see it. It is done to be seen in the time. It is not done to be transferred into some other place and to some other scale. Architecture also has the dimension of use and occupation. And I, too, do not want this discussion to generate into whether architecture is art or not. But very often it is used as an excuse. I can remember people saying, "but your drawings, they are so artistic, they are art" and I recoil from this statement, I think they are architecture, they are within the framework of architectural culture, even though they might use art strategies.

AARON BETSKY

If we don't want it to be called art, because as Andy Warhol said, art is a man's name, what do we want to call it then. Is there anyone else who has got any suggestions. We heard all the theoreticians, including myself and Xavier this morning, do any of the architects want to venture an idea about what it is that we should name this or pin-point this latent utopian character, I am fishing around for...?

XAVIER COSTA

(... feedback-signals make it impossible to understand Xavier Costa...)

AARON BETSKY

We are losing momentum here! I think, we were just arriving at a very interesting point where we were trying to get a little bit closer to what it is, that these various architects here are doing. Not that it is the "sum-total" of their work, not what it is that they are doing to fulfil programmes or to make money or to even have a social effect, but there is something that they are doing that Patrik and Zaha thought was worth putting into this exhibition called "Latent Utopias". Something that addresses various issues.

The discussion continues in panel B:

STUART VEECH

One thing that is interesting is the idea of research, but it is collective research. And the idea Ross was talking about, that work in Hollywood, and the idea of film industry – there is a huge amount of possibilities, of cross networking, and I think it is a collective research and collective testing, of our experiments, it is going to begin a revolution as to how to realize these things.

ROSS LOVEGROVE

I have been really interested in what you said. You are one of the few people who brought the issue up of how to go from what I call ethics kit culture to something that is built. And what I mean by ethics kit culture, for any of you who build ethics kits, you'd receive a present in a large box, with the picture of an aircraft-carrier on it, with a beautiful image, and you open it up, and there are some plastic parts that you do have to create that thing with. So, there is always a huge disappointment with what you see inside. In my everyday life I am involved in trying to elevate the authenticity of products, that means that what you create, ultimately represents that dream. So you don't disappoint people. So I actually do not use a lot of computer images to show people, because the final thing just disappoints. I am very honest in my use of technologies and I am very

selective. Architecture is enjoying this wonderful free fall at the moment and I am very seduced by – I think there are wonderful things going on. There are all these wonderful sculptures out there now, but when it comes down to the reality of how to turn those into an industrial construction, you're going to be faced with questions, that I am faced with everyday. I mean, The Emperor and his clothes type questions, where people say... "why are you doing that, you are using four times the material, it is four times the cost, it is the worst method of construction it does not give you a good enough structure", and I say, "hey, but it looks funky", but that is not good enough. And in my world, well, the world I circulate in, I see so many people, psychopathically drawn in to celebrate things which are irrelevant. There are things that look modern, which are fundamentally not modern. I would like to see a little bit of that thought come back into architecture... you know, for years I followed the work of Kaplitzky and Future Systems, because I thought the guy was following something that was sort of scientific and structural and the whole thing. And then suddenly he is been gripped by fashion, and he is throwing that all away. There is no logic in it. And I..., you know, if he had built Bilbao out of solar panels, it would look better than out of titanium, it would look much better, and have roughly the same cost, well you could get someone to support that. If you start to combine beauty and logic, you get everything that you see in the exhibition here. And more. I just don't see from the outside, as an observer, that there is enough effort that goes into technologies.

And again, in my field, if you can't get a company to support your vision fully, you often shift to another vision. If you look back ten years at the work of Inflate – Nick and all those guys – they came out of the Royal College without any money, they wanted to build some things, so they used the cheapest methods possible. Polystyrene, they took inflatable structures, and they created some really fantastic things from nothing. And it is interesting to see in an exhibition like this, if you look at the work of Greg Lynn, who I think is really pioneering this idea of technology related to sciences and technology. There is no reason why they could not be built in polystyrene. They should not be just a suggestion. It could become a reality. And I mean in my studio we have discussions about how to build polystyrene buildings, because they are light, transportable, they cost nothing, they are insulating, they are waterproof, and then we turn around and say: well, what happens if the surface comes off? and we say: could you iron it with an iron to seal the surface or could you spray something, or do you leave it to pixeling, like foam on a beach, which is actually very beautiful. I mean a polystyrene building will probably take 300 years to blow away, and if it was recyclable polystyrene, that is fine. Just goes like the mist into society. So, you need a little bit of lateral thinking in that you can not build skyscrapers in that way, yet. But there are only a few people in the profession I see, who are trying a few of these things. And I think, there should be much more of a connection between these parts. If you talk to Miyake about clothes – I mean, he will never stitch anything together ever

again. This is a hell of a break through, now. If you put glazing on a building, could that be a way that you use a thick cling film, that means you never have to bond a piece of glass ever again. I don't know, but there should be a bit more on the experimental level expressed in perhaps another exhibition, which is called "Science and Experimentation", not necessarily "Latent Utopias", because, when I started this project I looked to all the solar things, and I did isometrical studies of transparent rotormoldings and I looked at the thing and it looked boring and it didn't satisfy my other desire, which is that of holistic, integrated, organic form, so I chose the second one, as something that satisfied my selfish desires, rather than my ethical desires for society, but hopefully in the future you could perhaps cover my form in some film that would be self-generating. So that's the way I comment on this, and I think that there could be more of a discussion on it – not necessarily now, of course we switched off to the other side so here we could talk about, if you want.

STUART VEECH

I think it's an interesting viewpoint that Ross has as a designer doing product design, because product designers generally have to deal with reality. They have to deal with materials, they try to figure out with new research on materials what kind of effects you can have. Architecture and architects generally have one major problem – that it takes too long. Your feedback, your response from the producers or the response from your clients or from the users are so slow. And in our work, we are bombarded. Anybody who knows the work that we have done for ORF here, we do the "Zeit im Bild"-Studios, we do a lot of testing in media-environments, we are always confronted with the issue for four or six weeks of completing the whole project. That means, a client comes to us and says he wants something, and we have to work with him to define the whole issue, to define the programme, to do the testing and we finish it within four to six weeks. And this is a kind of an insane situation, but it forces you, very quickly, to make decisions and to see how flexible we can be with using materials and creatively using materials, whether it is scaffolding, that you are cladding and scaffolding it's not necessarily a very complicated machinery that you need for it and I think that has become a very important topic – creating complicated architecture, maybe visually complicated architecture, with very simple means and I think this is something which is not happening right now. I think this is something that architects have to look at.

XAVIER COSTA

Well, I think that we have gone from an initial interrogation this morning, on the notion of autopoiesis as it has been posed by Patrik Schumacher in the catalogue of the exhibition and the introductory text which opens up this question of how the discipline and the context of architecture are balanced, one in relation to the other. I think this second session has clearly been directed towards interrogating these boundaries of the profession, not only in regard to how the work of the architect necessarily has established a network of collaboration with other areas of research and production, but we have also talked with designers, who have told us about their work and about how certain aspects that come from outside of architecture can reconfigure our direction, our horizon. I think that we have to take a break now, we will try to re-establish the connection with the upper room, hopefully that will happen, and we'll start with the third table in a few minutes, thank you.

Space Condition Part 3

Michael Speaks with
Zaha Hadid (Zaha Hadid Architects),
Bill Mac Donald and **Sulan Kolatan**
(Kolatan / Mac Donald Studio), **Brett Steele**
in location A

Neil Leach with
Mark Goulthorpe (dECOi), **Farshid
Moussavi** and **Alejandro Zaera Polo**
(Foreign Office Architects), **David
Erdmann, Marcelyn Gow, Ulrika
Karlsson** and **Chris Perry** (servo),
Tobi Schneidler (interactive institute
in collaboration with servo)
in location B

NEIL LEACH

Let's make a start. Welcome to the final session. My name is Neil Leach and I have the privilege of chairing this, it has been deliberately put together as a finale … the best at the end and I think it is a very interesting panel. First of all, as you can see, we are not connected with upstairs. This allows us to focus on a particular sort of question. The theme that has been put down is the theme of digital tectonics.

MICHAEL SPEAKS

… for me it would be really terrific and instructive and interesting – oh, we have them and they are listening! – to first hear from Zaha Hadid about the exhibition, about, maybe in some ways, what it means and about…, whether or not "Latent Utopias" is another way to say other kinds of things in contemporary terms. I suspect and I wonder if, in fact, it is not a way to talk about something else, something always possible. Zaha, you said: "Everything is possible." So in a way everything is possible is a way to restate the idea of latent utopias. And I am wondering if I am even close with that.

ZAHA HADID

I remember very well in my fourth year at the AA, when I discovered that everything is possible and given certain tricks you learn and obviously a craft, but many years later, when I was lecturing in Germany, someone came up to me and said: "Isn't it a bit kind of 60ies to think that everything is possible? Is it because you are Iraqi that you think, that progress is possible?" I think at this current moment it is particularly interesting that an Iraqi thinks everything is possible. And I think without really the ambition that I pursued and many others… Nigel, and those who are with me at the school, it is a particularly strange panel, because I know all of them extremely well, Bill Mac Donald was one of my firsts students at the AA, he kind of suffered my ignorance in teaching and the first experiment on being a teacher and a student at the same time. And this is also a part of the utopian ideal, that you do not really know, but thinking you know everything. So somewhere at the end Brett Steele, he also was sort of an end-up-to-student – he never really joined the pack, he joined my office in 85. Sulan has also been a very close friend of mine for a long time. So, I think this show is also amongst friends and colleagues. I am wearing many hats today, as a curator of the show, as an architect and by the way, I could not call myself an architect until very recently, because I was not registered, because at the AA we were taught, we were encouraged, let's say in the 70ies, when most of you were not yet born, that, well, I am one of the old crowd in this show, and I am not scared to be amongst young people. So, this is also a part of the utopian ideal, that there is no difference and that we have to learn, to a degree, a generosity to accept difference. I have to say I have really suffered and I don't want this to seem like a…, I mean, I was whipped, let's say, because I did not conform and it wasn't because I wanted to be a rebel continuously, but I really thought there was an open window for me in the late 70ies, that with a bit of ambition, with incredible vigour, one could achieve the ultimate utopian project. And I think, this is what this show is about, I will take a point which Nigel mentioned, maybe he did not say it explicitly, that there is not enough dirt in the show. I don't mean dust. I mean, in the terms of being kind of avant-gardist and ambitious, that it is too clinical, somehow, it's going to be over washed. So maybe at the end of the show it might achieve the degree of slumniness, which can actually make event spaces possible, because I think that architecture, as a kind of formal language alone can not achieve that ideal, that I think, that integration of products and economics, and a kind of social idea, as what makes it possibly an accident. And I thought by the preparing of the show as a part of the ambition it can achieve some of this really kind of unpleasantness and…, so anyway, I think that to go back to this idea, that I think that in my professional career there has been no moment closer where art and architecture and all the other mediums like graphic design come closer together and trying to bring a building on that ultimate theoretical level.

And as a teacher, I think it's very important to – and as a student – know, that if you keep the door slightly open, you allow many layers of thinking to occur and have a kind of enlightenedness and make us better people and ultimately, I know the Americans sometimes disagree with me on this, not necessarily you, but the older Americans, that architecture is not only done for it's sake but it's actually done for well-being and for the social agenda in mind that for ultimately these environments that have been translated… to deal with their special experiences which can enrich various lives, as it is really our goal. And on the

level of larger to smaller scale that these are triggers – in a way we are going to try to wake the appetite or the taste of the people to see what could become – on a larger or a smaller scale – an environment. I don't want to take too much time, but I am really thrilled that the show has happened, of course I want to thank Patrik, and I will talk about the opening, because there're some funny moments, and Peter Oswald, who is not here, who really allowed us without much interference, or hardly any interference, to invite the people we wanted, but there are many others, who I would have liked to have in the show, who, some of them, refused, or could not make it, and the others, who did not make it this time. They will make it another time, one still has priorities. Anyway, it has been a great experience for me, anyway, and I think it is also important to be able to wear many hats and to achieve many – I don't want to call it dreams, because in Germany, in the German cycle, if you are not totally pragmatic, you are dreaming, and in England it is called wanking. And so between the dreaming and the wanking, and all that, I think that, I must say, in moments of absolute calmness and total hysteria, I have enjoyed the last 20 years, despite this difficulty and I said earlier I was punished for it. I think I would have been punished much less, if I were a white male. But anyway, the kind of whipping came very easily. It has been difficult, but also extremely worthwhile for me and I do believe in two things: exhibitions and competitions. Because these are the only things, through which I have been able to get anywhere. I am not part of any network. And also I do not believe that only built work is worthwhile. I think it is very important to allow younger people a platform, a place to operate and show their work and their ideas. And without giving this platform, I think we are only kind of making sample boards.

MICHAEL SPEAKS

Maybe we could turn quickly 'cause I'm still not sure if we are connected but if we could turn, if you can hear us, if you would indulge us and let us hear quickly from two students who have suffered at the hands of Zaha, maybe...

ZAHA HADID

One, one student.

MICHAEL SPEAKS

Ah, one – Bill, well, maybe you could – if you want to approach the issue of utopia, or – he can go.

BILL MAC DONALD

I'm trying to get, who's a student in this town and I can't...

SULAN KOLATAN

There are quite a lot of them!

BILL MAC DONALD

Actually, there are some here as well..

MICHAEL SPEAKS

I was all with you, Bill.

BILL MAC DONALD

Well I can answer maybe also as a student, even though that was 30 years ago, because I am

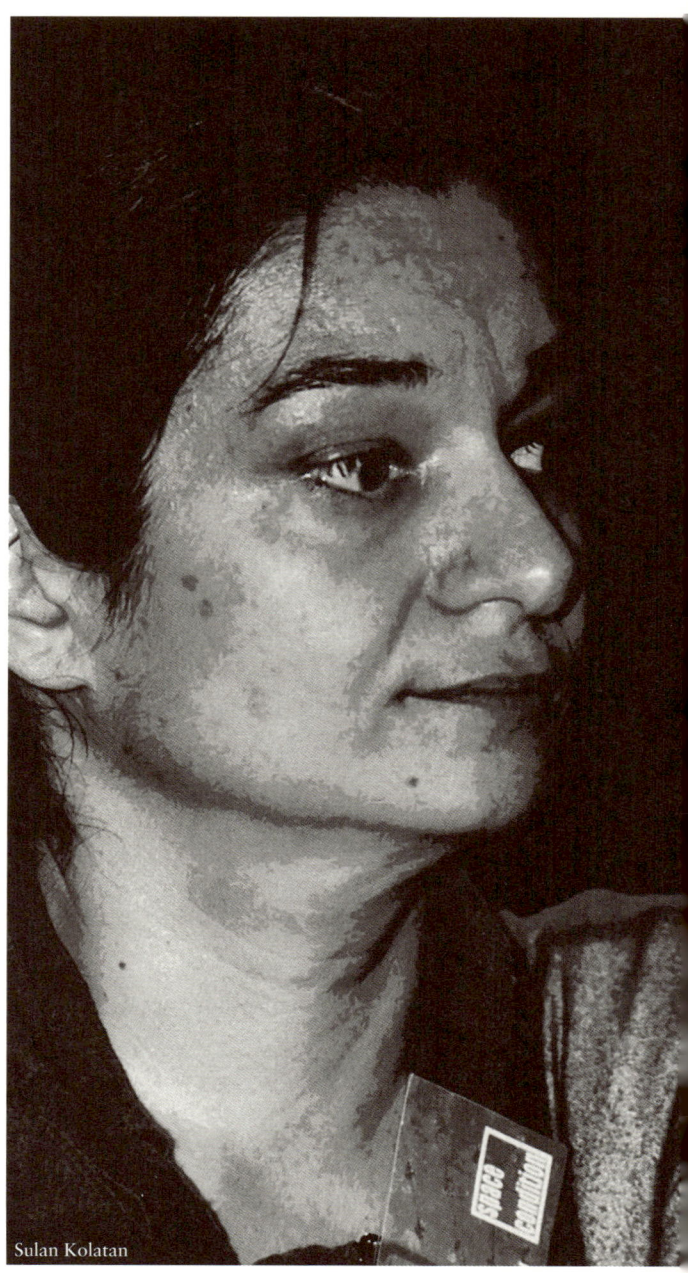

Sulan Kolatan

Bill Mac Donald

also still teaching, I think teaching in a certain way allows you the luxury of still being a student. One thing I had to say: When we were invited to this exhibition, we've known Zaha a long time and I was terrified, that on the decals for the names inside the exhibition she would use the nicknames, that she has for us. So, now I'm sure, they are not there, but what I would say, and I guess the question is about latent utopias, but what I was raised with in the title, was the term 'latent' or 'latency', which suggests a sort of impossibility, of a retaining that multiple utopia and then we were thinking about these kinds of conditions of imperfection and what was very striking to me was, actually on the plane here, in the "Herald Tribune" I was reading a review of a play now in London, but the review was not in the normal theatre section, it was actually found on the editorial pages of the "New York Times", written by E. Cohen and it's a play by Tom Stoppard, "Coast of Utopia", and it breaks down into really the 19th century rush and terms of how it transformed. It breaks down to three separate segments, much like this performance today runs over the entire day with middle breaks between and establishes itself in terms of the first section being "The Voyage", the next section "The Shipwreck" and the third section "The Salvage". And it's trying to make a relationship to ideology for the sake of ideology. And the difference of someone thinking that one of the quotes of one of the characters was "freedom is a state of mind". And the response by one of the other characters to that was, that freedom is actually not having the doors locked. And somewhere in between there, I think, our performance here today is where the exhibition exists. And there is a kind of unlocking of doors which Zaha mentioned, which I think is very important to maintain the continuity of keeping it open. So with that, something I refer to, what I thought was a team, running through some earlier presentations, was this question of ideology, and I think in some instances, all of us, we always confuse design-ideology with design-methodology. And in our current situation, it seems only natural to reject ideology for practicable theories, rather than practicing theory or in fact designing theory. I'm hoping that, maybe this is a kind of offering to begin a discussion in terms of how the distinctions in architecture today might be better understood as a collecitve, because I think there is a kind of collective here and that collective is in pursuit of particular design methodologies, away from design ideologies, in the hope, that something is produced.

MICHAEL SPEAKS

We're going to try to move around the table quickly at least to get an opening statement from everyone. Maybe I could ask both, Sulan and Brett a question that follows in some ways, the one that Bill asked, because earlier today I made a very general assertion, that, if modernism was driven and dominated by philosophical discourse and postmodernism, that is a sort of architecture and architectural discourse, was driven from, let's say, the sixties and till the mid-nineties by a theoretical discourse, that we are in the midst of some other kind of intellectual dominate, which I call design intelligence, and one of the things that strikes me

about the work that everyone at the table does, but in particular about the work that both you all and the work that has been done at AA-DRL has in common, is that both are steeped in a kind of intellectual approach to architecture and well, both I think, are driven by an interest in developing intelligences that are inherent to the practice and that name it. They are not driven by, what you are calling ideology, but what I would call theory and maybe you could both say something about that, because I think in fact both are innovative in the way that I described it earlier without searching for the new, which is old, perhaps, we'll see. Maybe you could both say something about this?

SULAN KOLATAN

Well, answering your question in a kind of a little roundabout way, I had an observation about the whole day today and I think it's a sort of, it's a kind of response to your question, which is that it strikes me, that even though the general thematic of today is utopias and innovation, that we have a tendency to fall back to defining our discourse with regards to existing definitions of categories. And by that, I mean, it struck me, for instance, that this morning there was..., these categories were posed as oppositions as it were, for instance this social versus form, or urban versus product. What I think is actually happening which is sort of close to the core of significant change, that we're in the midst of, is the fact that because things are being connected in ways, that are quite unprecedented, we really have to rethink from the get go the definitions of these inherited categories.

What I'm trying to say by that is, for example, I think it was Tom who said earlier that actually interdisciplinarity is a very old notion, there is nothing terribly contemporary about that, which is true of course, but the kind of interdisciplinarity, that exists or that is possible right now, is of quite a different order, I think. And it goes back to, in my mind, to the fact, that..., or it has got a lot to do at least, if not exclusively, with the notion and the capacity to connect many disciplines at the level of generation, through digital technology. For example, that we now have the possibility and we do use certain kinds of software that are common between disciplines, in other words, we as architects use for instance software that is actually made for a different category. And in the same way it's also true that output-technologies, production-technologies are establishing some kind of linkage now, where the same kind of machinery and tools are being used to output product-design as well as architectural elements. And the third component in my view is material innovation, new kinds of engineered materials, which are coming into being. They are actually developed for other fields but they are becoming more and more available in architecture as well and I think, the combination of the three really signals a very, very significant paradigm shift, both in terms of architectural discourse and theory as well as architectural practice. And with that also, I think, that it begs our questioning of existing categories of urbanism, product-design, architecture and even questions of, for instance, organic biology and so on and so forth and it sort of presupposes in some way, that this convergence at the root, in terms of technology and materiality, is a possibility for cross-platforming, that digital tools in themselves suggest a kind of cross-platforming between different disciplines, both in terms of practical output as well as theoretical discourses.

MICHAEL SPEAKS

Thank you – Brett:

BRETT STEELE

I think just to make a brief first response to your question about what may drive the work we are trying to do at the AADRL and what might distinguish it maybe from others, at least within that environment we are a kind of graduate studio for asserting, for doing the work. I would agree whole heartedly with what Sulan was just saying and I think a lot of other people today probably talked about it, which is the idea of work being driven by a kind of collaborative impulse across disciplines in ways that today are much more immediate, than maybe a generation ago, and about a work that was trying to focus on – what was at the time called a kind of autonomous architecture – architecture about architecture by architects for architects. And as Michael was describing this morning as a kind of critical agenda and what work was presented in relation with previous predecessors within the discipline. I think the collaborative impulses absolutely at the root, maybe of the kind of pieces, the installation within this show... but I think more than just the collaborative aspect, it is specifically the technologies of distribution that light the heart of this kind of sensibility. The fact today, not just that architects work with other disciplines, which I think they have done for a very long time, and I think schools like Bauhaus are still interesting nearly a century later, in part for architects working alongside advertisers in the original formation of the school, multimedia artists, or what at that time was taken to be multimedia and people in other disciplines. I think that kind of collaboration has long been in place. What is slightly different maybe in an area we are very interested in and exploring in the studio, is the way in which the thing we call an architect, and it is very much a kind of thing today, exists and operates through systems that distribute design across not just disciplines, but hardware platforms, software applications, and the actual network, where these projects emerge in the studio. We in the design of the AADRL five years ago – one of the things we were interested in doing was actually provoking to a degree the consequences of those networks, to the point that we shifted away from the idea of individual students or designers, being trained in individual productions, so that all projects have been done and these installations we have put into the show today, are occurring across teams of people, that are usually three, four or five at a time, which have a lifetime that runs through the length of the studio and in some way in addition to a kind of group-teaching, that occurs in it, projects simply emerge out of this kind of a setting of distribution. That we literally kind of lose the control, that might characterise ways in which architects and others have "designed", so to speak, in the past. These installations that we're including today, if we were to describe a kind of a

latent aspect or fascination we would have, it's probably in the latent possibilities of those kinds of connective technologies being used today as a kind of design space for the making of the projects.

MICHAEL SPEAKS
Neil, shall we try and work across platforms at least from above to below?

NEIL LEACH
The scene here has been set very well by the discussion upstairs, for having precisely the sort of debates that we were interested in pursuing in this group. And that is precisely the kind of new forms of collaborative practice that have been enabled in part by new technologies, by digital computer programs and so on, but also through kind of new working-processes, new operations in terms of both practices and here I am referring to the work of servo, who operate as a network, as a collaborative across different continents in a very imaginative and productive way, but also to the way in which members on this panel have been operating, breaking down the barriers, between what architecture might be and other domains. A kind of sympathetic liaison that is embodied for example in the work of Mark Goulthorpe's projects, is it architecture or what actually is it ? The work for example of Foreign Office Architects, their ferry terminal, which – it seems to me fools architecture in a number of different concerns, landscaping, structural, construction and so on. And we're getting a new paradigm of working which has been established. And I really want to ask each of the people on this panel individually just to say a few

words in the manner of the panel upstairs on this particular question, about these new forms of process, the new operations that are happening as a result of this new paradigm shift.

Just to introduce you to the people on this panel. On my far right Mark Goulthorpe of dECOi, Farshid and Alejandro of Foreign Office Architects, I have all four members of servo on my left, which is a rare occurrence, Ulrika Karlsson, Chris Perry, David Erdman and Marcelyn Gow, and to make up the team, in the spirit of this interactive operation Tobi Schneidler of the Interactive Institute, who has been collaborating with servo. So I want to start perhaps with Mark Goulthorpe.

MARK GOULTHORPE

I guess I'll start by tracking back the notion of utopia. … this latency…

MICHAEL SPEAKS

Mark, we can't hear you. Put the microphone as close to your mouth….

MARK GOULTHORPE

I think, inherent in the notion of utopia is the issue of design. And for me it is obviously, that utopia has not been an idle dream, it has been a program for rational improvement of man's condition. So I think fundamentally, the notion of utopia is linked to the scientific rationality. Whether back in Thomas More's Utopia, or early 20th century, when there was a mandate certainly to simply improving basic human condition. To design a utopia seems to be linked, and yet… we are in the what is called the

"design society", but I think, the notion of design we talk about, picking up on Bill's comment, is very different to that kind of scientific, rational mandate. The design in the culture we are living in, is one of ornamentalism essentially and pleasure, I think the basic tendency of utopia and utopia in the first half of 20th century has been essentially tended towards clothes, warmth, food. And what we are seeing is a mutation of the basic notion of design, and I think we find ourselves increasingly not proposing a sort of scientific, rational instrumentalism, deterministic models of operations, but simply open ended design speculations, to see what effects they release. I think we should not be trying to dismiss object design or formal design and differentiate it from architecture, I think we should simply recognize, we live in a design culture that operates, with all the objects and things around us functioning, very powerfully so and perhaps what is required is almost a social aesthetics to emerge. Aesthetics traditionally is linked… is something inherent within an object. 20th century aesthetics begins to think of aesthetics in social terms that an event or an object becomes aesthetic when a group of people sort of identifies through it. And the design culture we live in today is one where we participate in social aesthetics everyday, operating through objects. Increasingly to this specific question of how we are operating the new forms of practice, I think the digital technologies that we have are allowing us much more open ended, speculative design processes, design methodologies rather than design ideologies, or whatever. One of the most startling things, that I recognize in our own practice, are the liberties that are offered to architecture, it's no surprise, that in both of the previous sessions...

ZAHA HADID
Mark, could you speak louder please!

MARK GOULTHORPE
...it hasn't been alluded to is, that the liberating intensions of technology for us and I think we're finding the impossibilities of collaborative practice, but also in the various methodologies within the office, extraordinary liberating potentials. When I came out of Richard Meier's office, and I worked in Norman Foster's office, from the outside I think dECOi was a deliberate attempt to try and set up a collaborative potential for praxis. And increasing there, I find there was a sort of allowing people within the office to pass from designing components like basins all the way through the fabrication. And I'm recognizing in a kind of open ended experimental, associative, collaborative praxis, that's coming in all those liberties of practice, which is perhaps not the utopian way, but it's certainly optimistic, and I enjoy that enormously to think through what potentials might come.

FARSHID MOUSSAVI
I guess I would support the discussions put forward on the importance of available tools today and therefore the possible experimentation that we can generate or we can pursue as a result, we as a practice have certainly benefited from the use of information technology within the work and it has

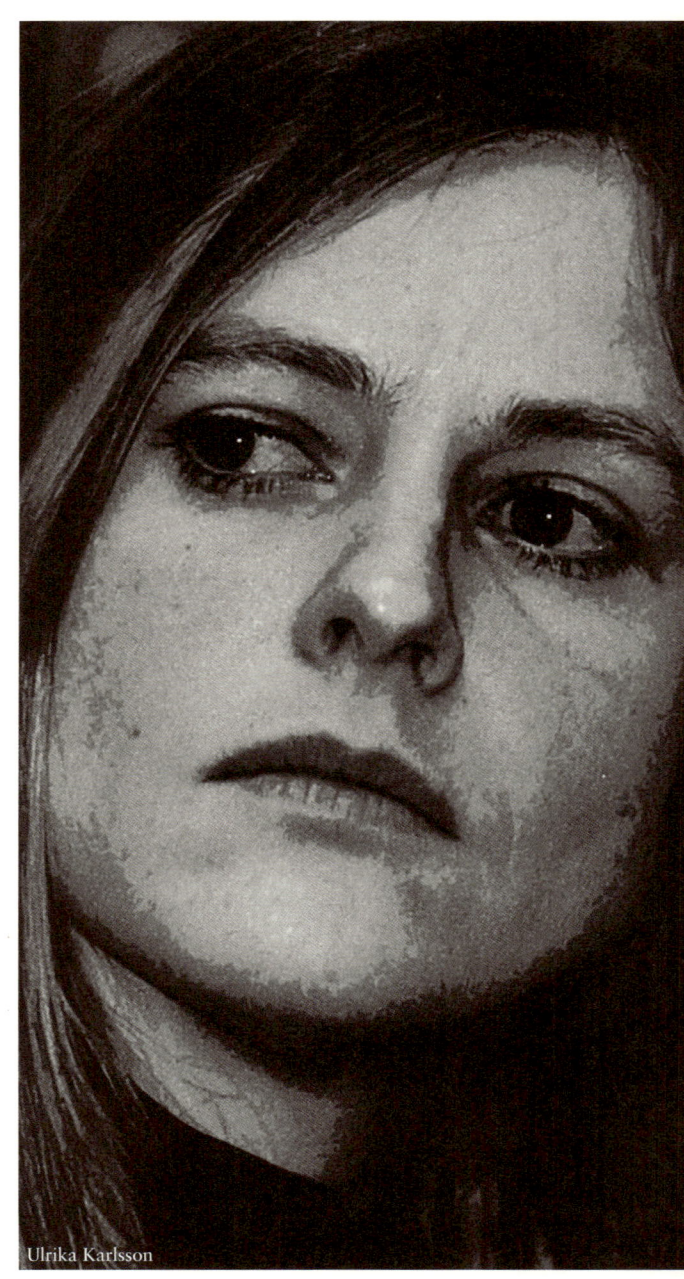

Ulrika Karlsson

Brett Steele

allowed us to open a design process, so that there is no longer an ideal of experimenting or producing ideas, utopian ideas that then need to be negotiated with reality. This is done every day, the design process is open to information of all kinds and scale and one is able to look for these virtualities, for these hidden potentials, if you like, while you practice every day. So that as I said you are not trapped in this problem of having to find possibilities for the ideas to be actualised, it is part of the everyday practice.

ALEJANDRO ZAERA POLO

I would just like to point back to the very interesting problem that Bill mentioned at the other table of utopia, as something that is related to the construction of an ideological position versus utopia, as the construction of a methodological position. I think that most of the people who are at least at this table, are very much part perhaps of the second one and I think that this is probably what we can try to do: to identify the potential reach of utopian thinking today. I think that the question Zaha and Patrik have put forward – "what should be the way in which we look at utopia today" forces us to question, whether the utopia in the traditional sense, which is the ideological sense, is still valid. And I would like to simply remind everybody, that utopia means literally "nowhere". So when one has to practice somewhere, probably the potential that you seem to encounter in a particular problem may develop, has to probably be exploited more through the deployment of a certain methodological approach than by the statement of an ideology. Whether the use of certain technologies implies an ideological position, which I think it does, is a different matter that is probably worth discussing here.

MICHAEL SPEAKS

Would you mind if I ask just a quick follow up question to that? You would mind? Ok, Ok. No I'm curious, just very quickly to ask Alejandro just the extent to which being involved in a global practice of architecture, because obviously everyone has used that word, to describe almost everything for the for last five or six years, but especially given the name of your office and given that you are all involved in a global practice, I wonder if there are inherent advantages to operating methodologically as opposed to ideologically I'm wondering. Specifically, if it doesn't have something to do with the fact, that if you work in different parts of the world, one can't assume, that a kind of specific ideology whether it's nation based, or based on a sort of theoretical proposition, or based on some kind of political position, if one can assume that that position gets you anywhere, when you practice in other places.

ALEJANDRO ZAERA POLO

I wouldn't say, that it makes a big difference. I think that the kind of ideological utopia is bankrupt. Simply because it's very difficult today to put forward an all encompassing proposition of how architecture should be. I think, that the fact that you operate locally or globally doesn't necessarily mean that setting or placing your utopia or your kind of practice on an ideology is more valid than putting your practice on a methodology.

I think that methodologies are also local. Not all methodologies work everywhere. I think that in some ways methodologies offer something that the same ideology has a certain locale.

NEIL LEACH

Can we go ahead? Yes I think, that this is a very good point to move over to servo, partly because they are a network that operate globally. I invited the whole team and I think for reasons of time I'll limit the time of the comments initially, to members of servo.

ULRIKA KARLSSON

Yes, let's continue the discussion on collaborations and networks. I think for servo it has been a necessity to have a dialogue and that dialogue has been made possible partially through technology. And it's interesting, that technology has been a social device for servo to have a continuous discussion. And so the practice is partly dependent on technology as a communication medium too – for the architectural work. Based in four cities, Zürich, Stockholm, Los Angeles and New York, it is obvious, and on this particular exhibition "Latent Utopias", we have also extended the network on a collaboration with the Interactive Institute and Tobi Schneidler of the Interactive Institute on the left here. Which also ties into this sort of interdisciplinarity that has been taken up earlier in the discussion. When dealing with a lot of advanced technology in the fabrication of architecture, through communication, inevitably, you're part of an interdisciplinary discussion and you also have to get help for getting into the dialogue, into discussion with people from other disciplines or the disciplines start to get blurred at the edges. So, who is actually the author of what? And, I don't know, if I should be brief here – I'll pass the microphone to Chris here.

CHRIS PERRY

Just to pick up on what Ulrike was beginning to talk about – can you guys in the other room hear me? Within this, Greg brought this up in talking about issues of authorship, within the framework of the AADRL, to what extent they actually work through teams, and begin to look at the complex distribution of authorship by setting up those kinds of collective infrastructures, and that's something clearly that we've been interested in, both the scale of practice, which is to say being a team of four, distributed across four cities in two continents, but also within a material itself, within the work. The interest being that it floats at a series of different scales and within that, I think one of the issues that comes up for us that is interesting in the framework of utopias, of latent utopias, a lot of discussions were earlier, specifically I think in the first discussion, when questions of experiment and research were raised by Greg, is an issue of intentionality, which is something that we've been looking at and, which is to what extent we can begin to visit questions of intentionality, questions of goal-oriented practice, meaning to what extent we could begin to complexify the kinds of optimistic or potentionally productive qualities of the utopistic phenomenon, which is to say somehow it refers to or conditions something which we look to, are on a kind of

idealistic platform, but complexify getting there through issues of intentionality which is to say problematising the assumption that one works, that one generates, both on the scale of practice, at the conceptional scale, an intellectual scale, the scale of research, as well as the material scale, through a goal-orientated procedure. I think those are some of the issues that come up when we begin to talk about collaborative practises, but also really raise a lot of instinct questions I think when we look at a global, sort of cultural phenomenon, but thinking about systems like Napster, to what extent those kinds of structures offer certain utopian qualities or performances, but not so much through a kind of goal-orientated intentional process, which is to say, they were quite emergent in a way. Their intentions weren't initially to threaten a kind of power-structure of the recording industry, but they actually unfolded a series of desires, desires built towards sharing, desires built towards a kind of self-awareness, in terms of how a new technology such as the internet could be deployed to set up potential collective systems. So, those are some of the general issues, and I think also extending into our work with the Interactive Institute, has begun to play in to what extent intentios further blur or paste our group into another group. It's been an interesting experiment, so with that I pass it over to Tobi.

TOBI SCHNEIDLER

I'll just be quick and introduce the Interactive Institute as a – we're basically a research group in Stockholm, composed of people from many different backgrounds, including architects but also engineers and artists. Now, we've actually collaborated a lot with – internally within these different disciplines, but also externally with companies, academic institutions and artists, for example. And the thing we found is, that it's really a matter of language, that needs to be addressed in communicating these new visions, these new inspirations, these new ideas about what, in our case for example technology and media, can have as an effect on design in how it is augmenting architecture for example, how it is augmenting artistic production but also engineering and theoretical work. Now, this matter of language is actually also important because it makes our work not just be confined to one of those disciplinary kinds of courts, I mean like, we're here today, like this kind of conference, where we all know our kind of context that we talk and operate in, but actually, our work always has to be able to address and to be understood in these different contexts and connect to different stakeholders. So, one crucial thing we found out is that we can't represent work any more in the sense that we, especially as designers, are resorting a lot to representational techniques, like discussed earlier. But we actually do prototype things, we need to do the real thing, even if it's in a different scale, than the actual thing, that we should be able to complete in a later stage. But experiences, that a project should transport, should be able to be transported in a model as well. And I think that was an interesting result that we achieved in this collaboration with servo as well.

NEIL LEACH
Ok, we haven't had the kind of disagreement, that maybe characterised some of the earlier sessions, but it might be interesting to get some feedback from upstairs, some questions from the group.

MICHAEL SPEAKS
No, we have none.

ALEJANDRO ZAERA POLO
I would like to point at one question that has been put forward to the table and which seems to be actually quite crucial in the discussion, which is the issue of goal-orientation or intentionality, because obviously, one of the things that ideology used to do was to set up the goals. So, if we are supposed to generate a certain utopia, which means a certain tendency towards something: is it interesting to have that goal? Because for example at this table, Mark was suggesting that media tends to actually dissolve directions or tends more towards open experimentation, while servo, or this morning Greg, seemed to be putting forward a sort of goal-oriented practice. I think this is a question, that is probably one of the questions that we need to answer, if we want to find a contemporary form of utopia.

MICHAEL SPEAKS
Could I maybe just expand on that and maybe offer a further comment? I mean, I don't know if people were here earlier today, but Greg Lynn made a distinction between his new interest in research and in a distant thing from experimentation and

following some of the comments from down there and thinking about what Alejandro just said, it seems to suggest that, and I think Greg said that then, that research was kind of end-oriented, which would seem to suggest that there is nothing really added. If that is the model of research and if that's the case, it seems somewhat problematic, it seems, if that is the case, then a return to thinking about utopia in contemporary terms would entail us rethinking the relationship between, for example, ideas that get completed in forms or even things like manifestoes, which get realised somehow, and I have to say that one of the things, I was most happy about in the publication, is that, despite the fact that the title of the exhibition and the title essay is called "Latent Utopias", that really is no manifesto as such and I wonder if – really thinking about this idea of rapid prototyping – if there is a way to think about making things as a kind of physical manifestation of a utopian thinking that is constant and that doesn't change. I wonder, maybe, if Zaha could say something about this, because actually there is a way in which the exhibition is an instantiation of – not a set of ideas – but of a position that one might be able to identify as utopian, but it doesn't have a manifesto as such and I wonder if you have any idea about this. No, nothing? But Bill wants to say something about this.

CHRIS PERRY

I just want to make a quick clarification, in terms of our position, because I think we actually – and Sulan was speaking about this in her opening statement – I think we're interested not so much in a dialectical condition, something separating goal oriented research from improvised experimentation, but in terms of some of the issues that were raised in the first discussion that we're actually interested in 'a third way' of sorts, a more synthetic condition that would somehow integrate the two, requiring the kind of intentionality that Greg was referring to when he spoke of research as necessitating an 'end', that which is goal-orientated or intentional... and at the same time would allow for the other extreme, that being experiment, or experimentation, improvisation... that which is somehow loose, open ended, and about the kinds of discovery which emerge from unintentional or non-goal-oriented work. I think we are really interested in this 'third way', this synthetic space which hovers between these two methodologies... again, research which is positioned between a space of intentionality and of unintentionality, that which is at once about focus and orientation, and at the same time very much about loosening up this focus and orientation in the very interest of discovery and invention. And I think it's this sort of space which is very much at the heart of questions regarding 'latency', whether one speaks of latency in the context of utopias or in the context of the creative process... in both cases one seems to read a simultaneity of intentionality and unintentionality... that which is latent exists, it is structured and present, and to that extent carries with it a kind of intention... but in being latent the intention we read is potential, meaning it hasn't been actualized yet. It's an interestingly ambiguous condition, and again, one which we feel is at the centre of any creative process, especially that which is collaborative and involving more than one person.

MICHAEL SPEAKS

Yes I think, Bill wants to answer that, but in fact if that is, what you're suggesting, it seems to be precisely what innovation is.

SULAN KOLATAN

I would say, that in our own work, research and innovation are sort of twofold, and they are a sort of mutually – there is – two directions are mutually affected, which – one is directly coming out of this question of adjusting design methodologies, I guess, relative to – I mean I feel, that in many ways, you know, Zaha was referring to pragmatism and the English, and there is a wonderful statement, that I read a while ago, and I think that it hits the nail right on the head, both in terms of characterisation, perhaps, but also in terms of our position right now, which is that the Frenchman turns to the Englishman and says: "Well it works in practice, but does it work in theory?" And I think, that this is a sort of – I find myself very much in this position right now, where being pushed as if it were to innovate or adjust to situations that are happening very fast and of which we are seeing a sort of a practical manifestation, almost as a kind of default condition. And so the question is, what does it mean theoretically and how can we theorize those situations and so for us, I think that is triggered partly by new tools and technologies. So when we do research we are trying to sort of perhaps literally make sense of these tools in the context of architecture and in a way, we're trying to use the inadequacy that arises out of that situation as a productive inadequacy, because I think,

David Erdman

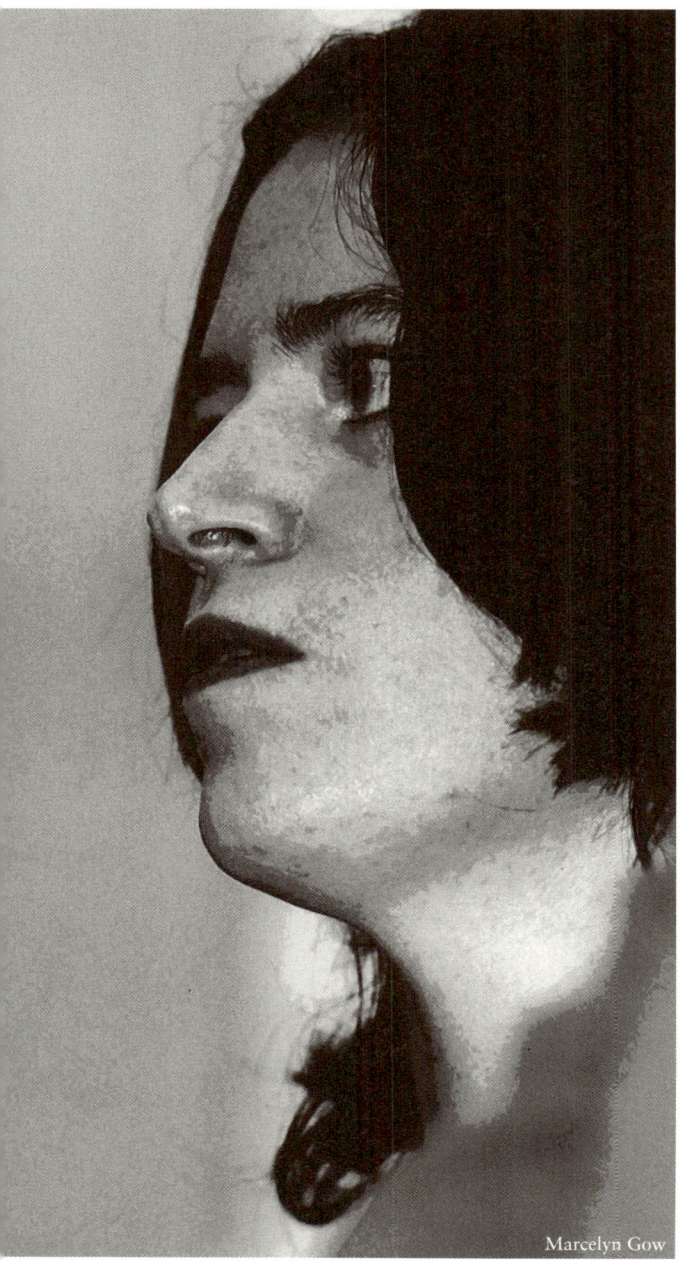

Marcelyn Gow

inadequacy, by nature, forces innovation. You can't fall back to inherited modes of operation and therefore you have to sort of not only solve the problematic at hand by innovating, but you also have to retrospectively ask yourself about the value of existing methodologies, I think. So that's one aspect of the research, but – and the other aspect I think is a kind of writing projective scenarios, writing scenarios about sort of potential realities and program-scenarios and to what extent there are sort of latent connectivities or affinities between new methodologies and new modes of thinking and operating and new kinds of living scenarios and programmatic scenarios.

MARK GOULTHORPE

I pick it up by – I was struck by servo's little comment of looking for some sort of mode of operation that is neither goal-oriented, a sort of deterministic research, but neither is it also the accident, and I think, there is not necessarily a contradiction in working in a non-linear, non-determinist way, it doesn't mean, you're working in a non-intelligent way. I think architecture is an active intelligence and we're in a period of latency, which is, you know for Freud, the condition of not yet having assimilated something, as we try to scrabble with these technologies, we are in a condition of latency, and I think what I recognize what's happening is, people are trying to sort of speculate intelligently, but in open-ended manner. So they're designing almost the possibility of architecture rather than a prescribed, a goal oriented architecture in the first instance. I think what's fascinating and again what I still find is liberating and to return to Zaha's notion of the dirt is quite delicious, whether it's casting something in bronze and finding – you know it retracts about five centimetres and doesn't correspond to the pure digital model, which is a sort of – form of – dirtiness, or whether it's a mathematician and an architect, trying to communicate and finding words like "elegant", mean completely different things in the two different domains. And there is a sort of delightful humour in working with a mathematician, when you sort of say "oh, could you make the wave more elegant", and he reduces the formula. And it's teasing out all of the kind of potentials of new forms of practice, that I think, what the real potential of latency is, which is a sort of finding, liberating potentials between all these sort of domains. And I think it's going to be a relatively brief period of kind of open-ended speculation, while we try to resimulate yes the latent quality of the digital.

MICHAEL SPEAKS

May I just put it together and ask if Brett would make a comment on that, because actually I think that one of the things that's really striking about what they do with the AADRL is, in an interesting way, I think they put together two of the models of intelligence production, I think that form the nature of the heart of a practice. One of which Sulan just mentioned, and that is scenarios, that is producing literally scenarios. I mean there is a whole range of intelligence production that occurs through construction of scenarios. And on the other hand, I think, there is rapid prototyping, in which form production is not production for a final

end form of product, but instead, in forms, techniques and cycles on itself ingenerates, in a really interesting, non-linear way, a kind of formal intelligence. So what is for me really compelling about a lot of the stuff you all are doing at AADRL, in a way you are putting these two things together. Could you say something about that?

BRETT STEELE

We have often tried to have an answer for the research question on the idea of how to marry the two terms in the lab's name, design and research, which are kind of juxtaposed next to one another. But one of the things we were interested in, with setting up the studio the way we did, was the idea of the way in which an approach to design as a form of research installs at some fairly immediate level the demand of seeing research itself as a design question. I think in the sciences one of the most popular books every year, is the book called "The Design of Research", which is the book most often cited by scientists in explaining the results of research that they undertake in their field. And it is a kind of classic text that all scientists have to buy earlier on to deal with the question of how to design a research problem, that is how you set the constraints. And it is very much an open-ended design question, how you can set the constraints in such a way, that a problem can be tackled as a problem and its results transferred across the working group – either that team or a larger audience within the discipline that is interested in the results. The demand of seeing research as a design problem, is the first way of breaking down this dichotomy that is often set up, that is that we have to pick research or design, and choose sides in the work. It is seeing the work as a kind of research problem, that then leads to this other area we have been interested in working in, which is the whole question of collaboration at a fairly, kind of straight forward technical level. That is, how do you literally let these projects develop across networks in such a way that people can actually work on them in some shared way? What we have is a kind of territory for this work as a group of people that come from all over the world, this year we got students from 33 different countries. In the 80ies students between the two phases, working in these teams, they didn't share a lot of things about the assumption of what drives architectural discourse. They come from very different local kind of definitions or experiences, of what constitutes the architectural project. One of the things that becomes interesting about the kind of shared territories that generation of people have today, are the really mundane things like C++ , HTML, Max-script, the latest version of MAYA, Microsoft 2002 Professional Edition, which becomes in a way, in a very real sense, the kind of medium in the most banal way possible, that those people are negotiating this question of collaboration. In a sense it is fully globalised and we might be an extreme case as a group of people that come – and 100% of our students come from overseas – but what this generation is working through in very real, direct and kind of mundane ways, is the way in which that way of working alone is inevitably a kind of research. I think, particularly about the splitting of the space through an interface. The interface becomes in fact one of the terms, that

maybe I'd suggest – might let us try to come to grips with the kind of complications that are introduced. I mean it is an amazing thing that everyone flies in today, and then divides into two rooms, just far enough apart, that the interface becomes the complication. How this event works, how a proposal was developed, has to negotiate these kinds of things today. It is not a kind of epistemological demand, it is not an idea or an interest, it is simply a real kind of condition.

ZAHA HADID

As only an observation – I think what I notice is that there isn't a discussion about a great utopian ideal. It is kind of many, many utopias, many ideals. And I wonder whether these – I don't want to call them fragments, because it is kind of an un-trendy word – these particles or pieces, will they ever form a great utopian condition or are they going to kind of fight against each other? And I think, it is very ambiguous, whether there is a friction between these ideologies or many ideologies, or there is a decorum. Whether it is an un-orchestrated condition, or totally orchestrated indirectly through the media technology. And I think, everybody is kind of – I find it slightly self-indulgent, and I don't think in the supposed ideal world, we were talking about a collective, I don't think that global makes a kind of collective thinking necessarily in this situation. What is the ultimate – even if we were to indulge ourselves for a moment – or the ideal goal? What is it, we are all struggling for, apart from many dreams or many ambitions. And I think, that – and what I think, I have been around long enough to notice, there isn't any longer a discussion about typology, that is dropped completely, so, there is no discussion about observation, when 500 students at the AA wrap themselves in something and try to kind of make a mark of what that means. So there are always kinds of methods or methodologies, these are methodologies..., when I went there there was sort of a discussion about that. But I don't know whether through these discourses we are trying to find what it is we are trying to change. Apart from the really heightened discovery of formal language.

MARK GOULTHORPE

I found increasingly, that – personally, when I am proposing a piece of architecture, there is an enormous barrier to this formal expert coming in and dictating something. And I confess, that my interest in parametric modelling and certain sorts of digital networking and exercises, has been to try and find a sort of new mode of praxis that would be less ideologically impositional. And the few tentative examples that we have had, of developing a parametric model that would give birth to a process but can allow all sorts of input to it. So you're designing, as to say not architecture, but with the possibility of an architecture, seems to me an extraordinarily powerful one, where, you know, the figure of the architect as this form maker begins to be a place within the technology, allows it to be networked and negotiated. And I find that those models actually managed to get a client feeling he is implicated within the design process and able to transform it to a certain extent, could be very powerful. The furthest we've gone is a sort of physical interactive environment where, really, at

the present, the architecture is nothing except the potential to respond the people, it is this notion of architecture as a reciprocity, which perhaps offers something, it is not an ideology of form that is being imposed, but it is a new working practice. That seems to me highly suggested.

MICHAEL SPEAKS

May I just quickly and maybe perhaps unfortunately suggest that we begin to move towards closure, or at least it has been suggested to me that I should suggest that. Does that make any sense? I am not saying "let's close", but Roger is telling me that we should begin to close. From up here Bill Mac Donald would like to make one point before we do and I do not know how you feel about – down there, Bill...

NEIL LEACH

I would like to get the two other members of servo for a brief comment at some stage.

BILL MAC DONALD

This will be truly generational since two of my former students are part of servo. I am going to comment on two issues they brought up I think. One is intentionality and criticality, in terms of joining the two together. And, what I think is a very important aspect, this issue of criticality came up in previous discussions as well, what I was going to say was that, at least for us, everything we theorize, we theorize with respect to practice and building, which is in a way, I think, the intention, and hopefully the goal. Everything we practice we also theorize. In a certain way this is an old thing, that goes some... the mother of necessity is the mother of invention. And maybe we should revise that given Michael's theme here, which is, the necessity is the mother of innovation. And in terms of that, the computer certainly I think – and software, that is his – afforded as the potential of looking at space in terms of time, form, space, program, – a sort of relative field of influence. And I think that also extends to the way in which we practice architecture today. I mean, Brett sort of established an interesting model of practice I would say, which has to do with design and research, and reminds me of a comment that was made to me either at the symposium or dinner after a symposium by Manuel Gausa who characterized the way that architecture has been practiced today as somewhat like an open GL-architecture, which is of course a computer term relative to a kind of Linux way in which practices operate in concert or in conflict. And I think what the strange thing about that is, that in a certain way each one of those conflicts and concerts propel the discipline forward. And the discipline is only propelled forward to this point if we allow for different roams of influence and spheres of influence that go beyond architecture, to allow us to invest not only ourselves in them, but allow them to be invested within us.

NEIL LEACH

Michael, can I please give over the microphone to the two members of servo, who have not yet made a contribution? David Erdman and Marcelyn Gow...

DAVID ERDMAN

I'll just make a quick comment that I think speaks to a number of the points that have been brought up. Speaking as part of the generation that is really using computers a lot to develop its work, I think, and also speaking to what Michael Speaks has alluded to a couple of times, which is the use of rapid prototyping. It seems to me that – relative to these issues of intelligence and how you begin to construct a theory around your work that..., at least for us there is a kind of built-in predisposition and repetitiousness to the way that we work being four people, which results from both the technology that we are using and the possibilities for its output. So the kind of optimism behind it is that through that repetitiousness and through beginning to rework things, and through – I think speed is not really the appropriate term for it – but there is a very loose relationship between what is happening on the screen and what is coming out of it. You begin to allow things to become, you know, a bit more inclusive in terms of building other people into that process, be they collaborators or clients. That ends up opening up that engine, or better cracking it open, to begin to be able to work with other people.

MARCELYN GOW

Yes, just to tie into that. I think something that has come up a lot in today's discussion, which is basically the issue of collaborative practice, and I guess I would like to flip it around and say, I am wondering what kind of collaborative reception a mode might be. I mean, it is something, I think, that both, Zaha and Nigel Coates alluded to, in terms of, you know, of introducing some aspects of the everyday, the grid, a sort of field in which the collaborative work does actually affect in – what one could term as the audience, but at what point does the audience actually enter that whole collaborative or responsive environment? I think it is definitely an emerging problem as the technologies are catching up with the – you know – the sort of theoretical and conceptual problems that are put on the table, that technology is actually able to enact some of them. So one would say, well, this might be something to celebrate, ok, that is the way those goals may be achieved, but I think, what is far more pressing for us to consider is, you know, what is that – or how this work is actually received and what are the new protocols for that reception. So I don't know if anyone would like to pick up on that.

MICHAEL SPEAKS

It is the first time I have spoken to Farshid and Alejandro since their extraordinary building's completion. It struck me there is one thing that Mark Goulthorpe mentioned earlier on: some things become suddenly unfashionable and that is kind of the question of pleasure in architecture. I think it's discourse, of kind of processes, it is a scientific, a kind of rational discourse, nothing of the body which Nigel Coates was talking about so eloquently is kind of left out, and yet, we find these extraordinary results of these very pleasurably, deeply extraordinary spaces and I think it'd be interesting to find out what sort of feedback the Yokohama has had from people who have been using it.

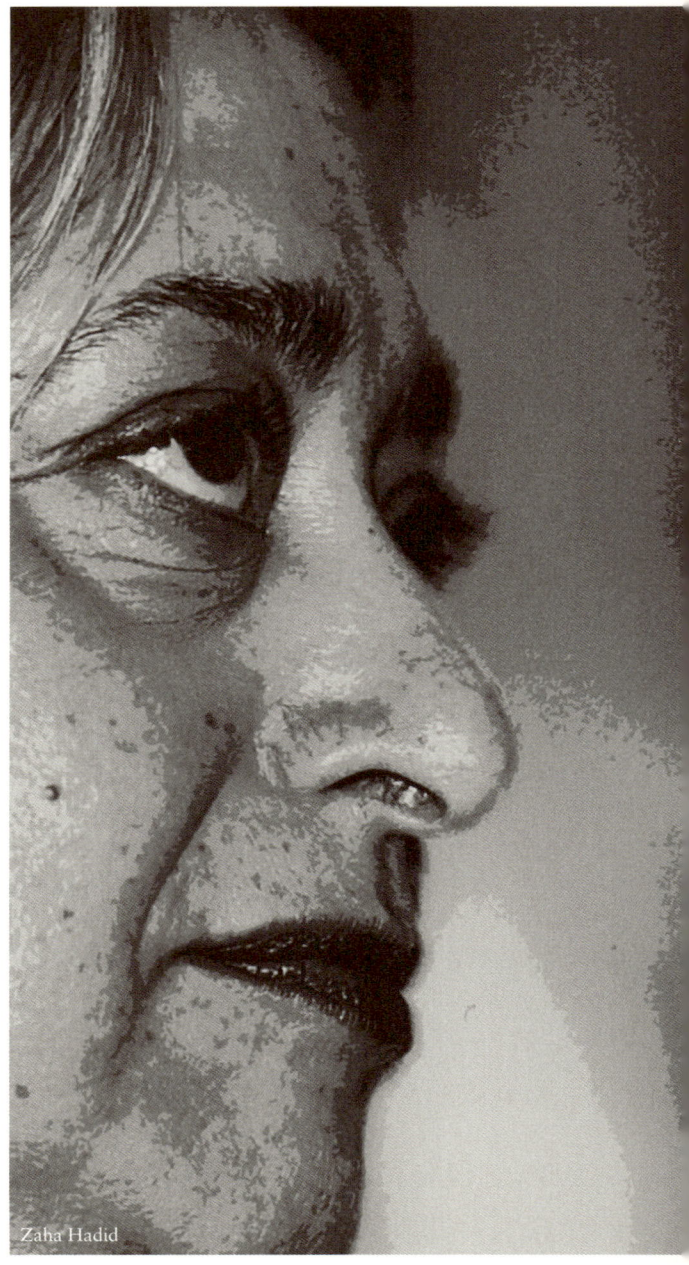

Zaha Hadid

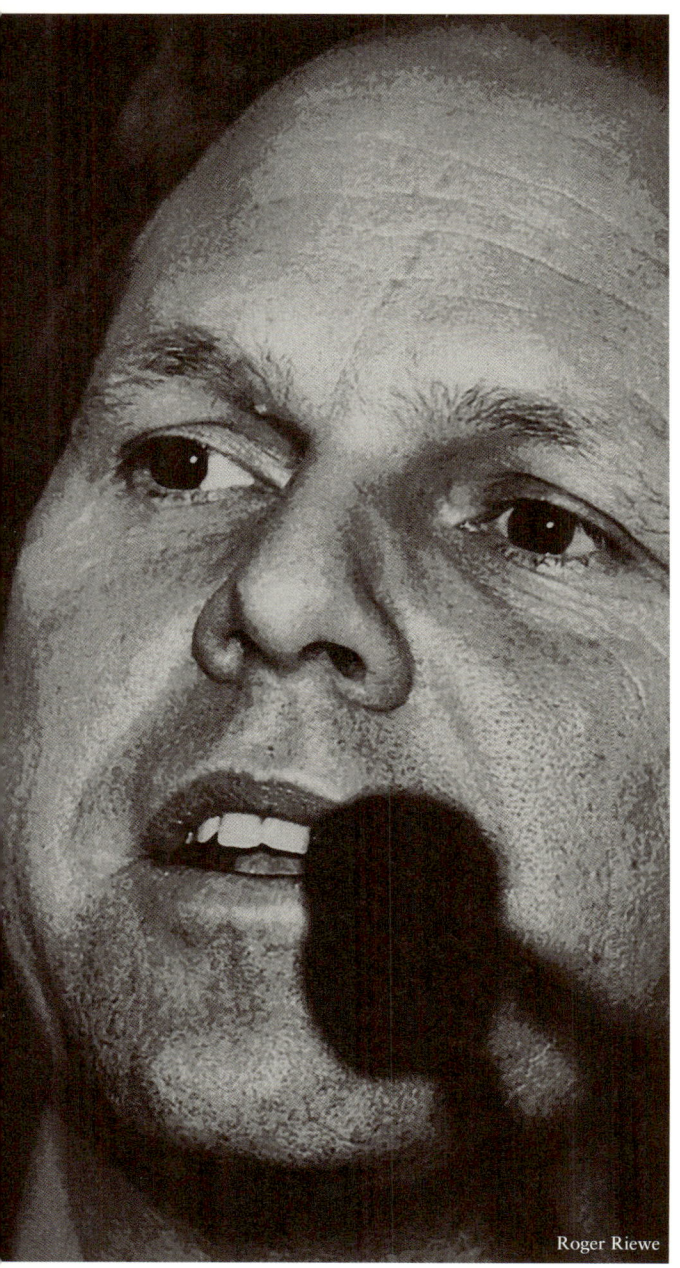

Roger Riewe

FARSHID MOUSSAVI

We have not had any kind of formal response, but all I can tell you is, that it was really very exciting to see on the opening day – we had a conversation earlier – to see how the Yokohama citizens, the Japanese had suddenly become foreigners in their own home land. There was an incredible sense of exploration, that somehow the space that they were exploring, was there for them to explore, that it was not prescribed to them, that it was a space of possibilities. And that is all I can tell you. We actually left after the opening...

ALEJANDRO ZAERA POLO

I would like to add maybe to the debate we are having, because I think it is a critical question, that if – there is something that is very interesting about this question of utopia today, at a time in which all of us work with computers, do biometric modelling, work collaboratively, etc. – what this question brings back is the sense for directionality. Now the question is, and now I want to review Zaha's words about the many utopias, a little bit of that idea that we need again to set up, at least locally in time and in space a certain directionality, because doing biometric models does not establish a direction. I believe, as an architect you need to set up the direction even if on the long term basis you do not know where it is going to end up, but at least locally in time and space you need to set up that direction. And I think that is perhaps what I would like to propose as a possible contemporary utopia.

MICHAEL SPEAKS

Sulan wants to make one quick point and I am being squeezed to make that the absolute last point. So please!

SULAN KOLATAN

I feel that I have to say something because I feel very hurt by Zaha's comment, that we all sort of have these minuscule utopias and that that all does not add up to much. I think that our generation's reluctance to define grand utopias does not prohibit us from participating in sort of working in directions which might have quite significant consequences. And I would like to just close with a sort of notion of a kind of collective utopia, which is sort of something like an urban ecology in the sense that the sort of man-made environment and all its elements, are converging with a natural environment on many, many different levels in sort of many different ways. And I think that I would say that all of our work in some way or another is located within that kind of notion.

ZAHA HADID

... on that critique I have to say. My question was not whether you are all... many in all ways, but that whether the collective of all these utopias would add up to a lot of thinking about what we call the city or whatever we might call it, or whether it does not. And whether there is a friction between them, and I think, that was more a question than a comment.

MICHAEL SPEAKS

I think that will carry on outside the panel, no doubt. We have just a few final closing comments from Roger Riewe, who was principally responsible for organizing this incredible day and some closing comments to make.

ROGER RIEWE

Thank you Michael and I am sorry, I have to be the bad boy now and close this discussion. But be sure, the show is going on this evening, a very exciting show. I am actually fascinated by this audience, being so quiet, so calm, listening so attentively, so this debate is for sure incredibly interesting. And I think there was also a necessity to open this debate and to have this debate here. We have now had about six or seven hours of solid debate, open debate, just to put certain points forward. The time, when we actually don't have these manifestos any more, and as you said, Michael, also in the catalogue, there are no manifestos, and there is a search for something else, instead, putting your point forward. The time is open, the time especially now, where everything is more or less politically correct, getting boring, there is the punch necessarily to actually put forward certain things to make life more interesting, actually open up new fields of architecture. I do not want to give a summary here, that would take another hour, and we should be off to the exhibition, but I would like to thank a lot of people, who made this venue possible.

First of all, my special thanks to Zaha and Patrik, because due to the fact that the "Latent Utopias" show was made possible, and has been actually set on stage here in Graz, we had the opportunity to set up this space condition symposium and I think the collaboration was very good, actually talking to each other, whom can we invite, who are the people in the show, who can we have here for the debate. And I think that worked extremely well, thanks a lot. I also have to express my special thanks to the steirischer herbst, and the Graz University of Technology, who actually financed this whole venue, this day. Which is actually also extraordinary, I don't think we've had a symposium of this size, so many people, in this building before today. So also this has been new, even the technology has been new, sorry for the brief mishaps, but – we have to try and next time we can have a conference in Tokyo, New York and London simultaneously, so this was the first try. Also thank you very much to the faculty of architecture and to the staff of my institute. And of course, this whole thing would not have been possible, if I hadn't had a fantastic team, supporting me. And I have to name them actually. For logistics it was Manuel Lebeda who has been around all over, for public relations it is Günter Koberg and multi-media it is Hans Grabner and

Herwig Baumgartner, for the videos Eva Grubbauer, Anja Jonkhans, Elisabeth Nöst-Kahlen and Hyewon Seo, for video support Peter Javurek and his team, corporate-design is Gernot Kupfer, and my very special thanks to, for support, organization, helping me all the time, Christian Kronaus. He's a great guy.

And of course this debate would not have been possible, had we not had these moderators here, helping along, actually leading this debate, taking part in it, putting points forward, and so on. Also I think, some new experience, because in our discussion yesterday, some of you were rather wondering, what would happen today, nothing really traditional, it is something new and I think the set-up worked quite well, so my special thanks to Aaron Betsky and Xavier Costa, to Neil Leach and Bart Lootsma, Kari Jormakka and Michael Speaks.

Thank you for being such a fantastic audience. It was a great pleasure having you here, the opening of the "Latent Utopias" is at 7pm and we will be seeing you there.

Thanks a lot.

GLEANINGS

We made it! Almost 8 hours of intense
discussion, which were followed with great interest
by approx. 900 visitors. It might have gone on
forever, but the "Latent Utopias" exhibition was
supposed to open on the very same evening. It was
a thrilling discussion in a set-up that initially
required some getting used to and yet, with time,
became rather stimulating and not at all a
disadvantage. Participants in the panel, who had
been sceptical initially, became active designers of
this to some extent seemingly anachronistic video
conference.

In anticipation of a future publication,
parallel to the panel discussion, participants who
were not part of the panel at the time were
interviewed with the intent of gaining further
insight into their position and way of working. Eva
Grubbauer, Anja Jonkhans, Hyewon Seo and
Elisabeth Nöst-Kahlen who carried out the
interviews, are all assistants at my institute and I
would like to express my grateful thanks for the
series of interviews that resulted!

Do we now have satisfactory answers to the
questions raised? Have we gained insight into the
architecture of the future? Did we enter new
territory?

Gleanings

Roger Riewe

SPACE CONDITION

ARCHITECTURE CONDITIONS SPACE.

The discussion was characterised by a
research-oriented working approach to which
many of the invited participants referred, and to
the way of working itself, which could be
described as supra-regional and trans-disciplinary
networking. The application of digital tools in the
design process and exploration of their range of
application obviously seem to lead to a strong
fixation on this medium and way of working

whereas many aspects seem still in their infancy in
this context. Not forgetting that this new world is
also welcomed with a certain fascination, which is
all too understandable. We also found out that
working with these digital tools forms an essential
basis for networking and the necessary
communication. So one could say that it is the
smallest common denominator. Indeed this aspect
has acquired special significance given that
communication in networking happens supra-
regionally, indeed globally. At the same time we
see that global topics will not become important
without the consideration of local contexts, and
that local problems can rarely be transferred to
other local situations. Therefore results gained

with networking can hardly achieve a sustainable position in the sense of de-localisation. The focus on new communication technologies and new design tools, as well as the necessary familiarisation with these new media, leads almost inevitably to some neglect of essential questions concerning architecture. The in-depth familiarisation with digital tools does also lead to intensive form-defining processes, leading to a not necessarily positive shift in topics relevant to architecture. Marie Therese Harnoncourt of next ENTERprise therefore quite rightly demanded that space be dealt with. Due to the effects of the use of new media in the design process and the exhibition title "Latent Utopias", the discussion on the conditioning of space was not a very deep one. The novel is always fascinating and thus, unintentionally, the essential things get neglected. It was therefore important that Alejandro Zaera

Polo pointed out that what is needed is a so-called "directionality", given that we architects, who are responsible for what we are doing, should also know what we want. Architects are still asked to give direction. Therefore, it seems important to me that, after a phase of digital-tool-focussed working and significant form-defining euphoria, it should now be possible to reinsert some essential themes into architectural discussion and deal with them again. These topics lie more in the political and social realm than in the area of form-definition itself. The answers are more likely to be found in everyday life than in one-off events. All in all it was both a very interesting and important discussion. As far as I know, never before had so many architects and theoreticians, working in similar fields, met in one place for discussion. Therefore, I would like to thank all participants in the panel for their commitment and contributions again. You all contributed to the great success of this event. Thank you very much! I think that, with the symposium "space condition", an important step was made toward pointing out paths to new architectures, but not necessarily to define a new architecture, which as such cannot exist. It represents experiments in contemporary architecture that should be seen and promoted as such.

Biographies

☐ ANGÈLIL GRAHAM PFENNINGER SCHOLL ARCHITECTURE – ZURICH – LOS ANGELES
RETO PFENNINGER

Founded by Marc Angèlil, Sarah Graham, Manuel Scholl, and Reto Pfenninger, agps architecture forms a type of alliance that could be characterized as a group-in-fusion, an expression describing aggregations of individuals linked by a common project. Individual authorship is questioned as design work evolves from team collaboration. The concept of the group-in-fusion fuses with the one of the subject-group, a term attending as much to the collective as to its constituent parts. The understanding of architecture as a collaborative enterprise suggests potential forms of interaction with professionals from other disciplines. Design propositions develop from a transfer of concepts and strategies located within as well as outside the domain of architecture. Beyond the traditional collaboration with consulting engineers and fabricators, cross-disciplinary relations are established with economists, biologists, linguists, psychologists and others. Within investigatory processes unexpected directions are pursued. Set standards of a prion established solutions are questioned and unprecedented approaches explored. Project team: Marc Angèlil, Sarah Graham, Manuel Scholl, Reto Pfenninger, Rolf Jenni, Philipp Hauzinger, Ursina Caprez, critical artist friend: Blanca Barer, manufacturer: Urs Meier (Luft & Laune GmbH)

☐ ASYMPTOTE
HANI RASHID

In 1989 Hani Rashid and Lise Anne Couture formed Asymptote, a design, architecture and research practice based in New York City. Asymptote has produced a number of key works in recent years that involve the use of digital tools and technologies in their conception and outcome Amongst the most important are the 3DTF, a virtual reality trading floor designed for the New York Stock Exchange and the Guggenheim Virtual Museum, a project commissioned by the Solomon R. Guggenheim Museum to incorporate and house their digital and Internet related art collections. Most recently Asymptote has completed the construction of HydraPier, a permanent building housing technology and art in Holland near Schiphol airport, an installation entitled Flux 3.0 MotionScapes at Documenta XI, a new line of office furniture for Knoll International and "Flux", a survey of their recent work published by Phaidon Press Limited.

☐ AARON BETSKY (Moderator)

Aaron Betsky is the director of the Netherlands Architecture Institute in Rotterdam. He is the author, recently, of "Landscrapers" (Thames & Hudson, 2002) and "Architecture Must Burn" (Thomes & Hudson, 2000). Previously, he was Curator of Architecture, Design and Digital Projects at the San Francisco Museum of Modern Art. Born in the United States, he was raised in the Netherlands and educated at Yale University. After graduating with a Master of Architecture Degree in 1983, he worked for Frank Gehry before setting up his own practice. Since then he has taught and lectured at numerous universities. He is also active as a writer and contributing editor to several design publications, recently in "reflect 01" the new magazine by NAI publishers and he is a member of the editorial board of GAM – Graz Architecture Magazine.

☐ BRANSON COATES ARCHITECTURE
NIGEL COATES

Nigel Coates was born in 1949, he studied at the Architectural Association. Coates and his partner Doug Branson began working together as branson coates architecture in 1985. Their first successful arena was Japan, where they built over twenty buildings and interiors. With their characteristic wit and cultural complexity, they succeed in summarising the Japanese aspiration to collect from, as well as seil to, the western world. Later they built many shops, restaurants and museums in Britain and Europe, including the National Centre for Popular Music and the Geffrye Museum, both in the UK. Coates has pursued research through exhibitions and publications of which "A Guide to Ecstacity" is the most ambitious. Furniture and glass designs have also won him recognition as a contemporary designer. He is Professor of Architectural Design at the Royal College of Art, London.

☐ XAVIER COSTA (Moderator)

Xavier Costa is an architect and writer based in Barcelona. He currently directs the

Metropolis Graduate Program in architecture and urban culture, and is curator of architecture for the Mies van der Rohe Foundation, also in Barcelona. His academic activity includes teaching at the Architectural Association, Columbia University, University of Pennsylvania and Barcelona School of Architecture. Publications include: "Habitats, Tectonics, Landscapes", with Michael Speaks, Ignasi de Sola-Morales, Ole Bouman (2001), "Wiel Arets: Works, Projects, Writings" (2001), "Fabricatlons", with Terence Riley, Aaron Betsky, Mark Robbins (1998), "New Territories, New Landscapes" (with E. Bru 1997), "Situationists. Art, Politics, Urbanism" (1996), "You Are Here: Architecture and Flows of Information", with Laura Kurgan (1996).

□ dECOi ARCHITECTS
MARK GOULTHORPE

In 1991 Mark Goulthorpe established the dECOi atelier to undertake a series of architectural competitions, largely theoretically based. Significantly, such work was presented under the rubric dECOi, which was intended to allow for the possibility of collaborative practice, and which has latterly become essential to a digitally-networked creative enterprise. Based in Paris, dECOi's portfolio ranges from pure design and artwork through interior design to architecture and urbanism. dECOi has received awards from the Royal Academy in London, the French Ministry of Couture and the Architectural League of New York, and has represented France at the Venice Biennial and the United Nations. They were selected by the Architects Design journal in its international survey of thirty "Emerging Voices" at the RIBA

in London, and were awarded second place in the BD "Young Architect of the Year" Competition, 1999. They were invited, as international representatives, to the Venice Biennial 2000, and to exhibit 10 years of work at FRAC in Orleans. Recently they were awarded the prestigious international FEIDAD Digital Design Award 2001, and invited to the 'Architecture of the Non-Standard' manifesto at the Centre Pompidou in Paris 2003. Design competitions awards: 2002 Venice Biennale The French Pavilion, Venice, 2001 FEIDAD International Digital Design Competition, First Prize, Taiwan, 1999 Gateway to the South Bank Competition, Second (Peoples') Prize, London, UK.

□ FOREIGN OFFICE ARCHITECTS
FARSHID MOUSSAVI,
ALEJANDRO ZAERA POLO

foreign office architects ltd, founded by Farshid Moussavi and Alejandro Zaera Polo 1992 in London, is an international practice of architecture and urban design dedicated to the exploration of contemporary urban conditions, lifestyles and construction technologies. Rather than specialising in a particular geographical area, scale or typology, the work of FOA has a trans-scalar, trans-national dimension, seeking out the possibility of innovation in a constant feedback between scales and cultures. Operating by mutation, displacement, migration, the work of the practice attempts to turn alienation, estrangement and foreignness into powerful creative tools. Currently based between London and Tokyo, FOA's emerging body of work ranges from large-scale urban proposals and

transportation projects to commercial and interior projects built in America, Europe and Asia, both for public and private clients. foreign office architects' major projects include: Yokohama international Port Terminal, Japan; Barcelona South-East Coastal Park, Spain; Municipal Theatre and Auditorium, Torrevieja, Spain; Publishing Headquarters, Paju, South Korea; Zona Franca Office Park, Technological Research Center de la Rioja, Cabo Rabos Tenerife and the BBC Music Centre.
Alejandro Zaera Polo is dean at the Berlage Institute in Rotterdam. Farshid Moussavi is Professor at the Academy of Fine Arts in Vienna and member of the editorial board of GAM – Graz Architecture Magazine.

□ ZAHA HADID ARCHITECTURE
ZAHA HADID

Zaha Hadid studied architecture at the Architectural Association from 1972 and was awarded the Diploma Prize in 1977. She then became a partner of the Office for Metropolitan Architecture, taught at the AA with OMA collaborators Rem Koolhaas and Elia Zenghelis, and later led her own studio at the AA until 1987. Since then she has held the Kenzo Tange Chair at the Graduate School of Design, Harvard University, the Sullivan Chair at the University of Chicago School of Architecture, guest professorships at the Hochschule für Bildende Künste in Hamburg, the Knolton School of Architecture, Ohio and the Masters Studio at Columbia University, New York. She was made Honorary Member of the American Academy of Arts and Letters, a Fellow of the American Institute of Architecture, and a Commander of the British

Empire, 2002. She is the recipient of the Pritzker Price 2004. Currently she is Professor at the University of Applied Arts, Vienna and she is the Eero Saarinen Visiting Professor of Architectural Design for the Spring Semester 2004 at Yale University, New Haven, Connecticut. Zaha Hadid is principal of her own office, Zaha Hadid Architects, in London. The first milestone building – the Vitra Fire-station – was completed in 1992. Since then a series of further buildings (Landesgartenschau 1999, Mind Zone 2000, Strasbourg Tram terminal and Carpark) have been completed and a whole series of larger projects are under way now (Wolfsburg Science Centre, National Art Centre – Rome, Central Plant Building BMW Leipzig and the Ordrupgaard Museum extension in Copenhagen). Recently the practice completed a design for the "One North" Master Plan in Singapore. The Studio is also working on a Master Plan for Bilbao's "Zorrotzaurre" district in Spain; a Master Plan for Beijing's "Soho City" in China and is on the final competition shortlist of architects to design the Olympic Village for New York City's 2012 bid.

☐ ERICH HÖDL
RECTOR GRAZ UNIVERSITY OF TECHNOLOGY 2000-2003

1962 – 63 Studies in Mathematics, Ecole des Arts et Metiers/Paris; 1963-68 University of Economics/Vienna, 1968-73 Scientific Assistant, Institute for Macro- and Structural Planning, Technical University Darmstadt; 1974-77 Professor of Political Economy, University of Kassel (Dean 1975-76); Member of Expert Group Environmental Research, Umweltbundesamt/Berlin; Consultant for

several Federal Ministries and EC-Commissions; since 1977 Professor of Economics at University of Wuppertal (Member of Academic Senate); 1978-79 Guest Professor at University of Vienna. 1987-91 Vice Rector for Planning and Finance in Wuppertal, 1991-99 Rector; 1992-99 Member of Senate and International Commission of German Rectors Conference/Bonn. From July 2000-Sept. 2003 Rector of Graz University of Technology; since 2001 Member of Styrian Council for Regional Development; since 2002 Member of Kuratorium of Styrian Future Fund, since 2003 Honorary Member of alumniTUGraz 1887, currently consultant.

☐ KARI JORMAKKA (Moderator)

Kari Jormakka studied architecture at the Technical University in Otaniemi and Tampere in Finland and he studied philosophy at the university in Helsinki. He completed his Ph. D. at the University in Tampere in 1991. From 1986-88 he was scientific assistant at the Technical University in Tampere, from 1989-95 he was assistant professor at the Ohio State University and from 1996-98 at the University of Illinois. Since 1998 he is professor for Architectural Theory at the Technical University in Vienna. He is also active as a writer and editor. His most recent publications include "Flying Dutchman. Motion in Architecture" in 2002 and "Geschichte der Architekturtheorie" in 2003. In 2002 he was editor of "Building gender" with Dörte Kuhlmann and of "Umbau 19. Diagramme, Algorithmen, Typen". Kari Jormakka is member of the editorial board of GAM – Graz Architecture Magazine.

☐ KOLATAN / MAC DONALD STUDIO
SULAN KOLATAN, BILL MAC DONALD

In 1988 Sulan Kolatan and William Mac Donald founded Kolatan / Mac Donald Studio. Currently, their projects include several private houses, an interactive travelling exhibition and a luxury resort, new furniture and house prototypes based on biomaterials. Sulan Kolatan, born in Istanbul, Turkey, received a Diplom Ingenieur degree from Rheinisch-Westfälische Technische Hochschule Aachen, and a Master of Science in Architecture and Building Design from Columbia University. She has taught architecture as a Visiting Professor at Barnard College, Ohio State University, the University of Pennsylvania, Parsons School of Design and as Visiting Critic at the Technical University Darmstadt. William J. Mac Donald, born in Milford, Massachusetts, studied at the Architectural Association in London, and received a Master of Science in Architecture and Urban Design from Columbia University. From 1985 to 1988 he was director of the MS in Architecture and Building Design at Columbia University GSAPP. Together with Sulan Kolatan his work has been exhibited and acquired by international venues such as the Museum of Modern Art in New York, the F.R.A.C. Centre in Orleans, the Deutsches Architektur Museum in Frankfurt, and the San Francisco Museum of Modern Art.

☐ NEIL LEACH (Moderator)

Neil Leach is Professor of Architectural Theory at University of Bath, U.K. He also teaches at the Architectural Association in

London. His research focuses on the interface between architectural theory and contemporary debates within continental philosophy and cultural theory. His most recent work is on the impact of digital technologies on architecture. Recent books include The Art of Camouflage (forthcoming), Designing for a Digital World (2002), The Hieroglyphics of Space: reading and experiencing the modern metropolis (2002), The Anesthetics of Architecture (1999), Millennium Culture (1999), Architecture and Revolution: Contemporary Perspectives on Central and Eastern Europe (1999), Rethinking Architecture: A reader in cultural theory (1997).

☐ BART LOOTSMA (Moderator)

Bart Lootsma (Amsterdam, 1957) is a historian, critic and curator in the fields of architecture, design and the visual arts. Together with the architectural historian Mariette van Stralen he founded V.O.F.Boiling Phenomena. He was a visiting Professor at the University of Applied Arts in Vienna, currently he is teaching in Delft and Nuremberg. He is an editor of ARCHIS, member of the Scientific Committee of ArchiLab in Orleans, curator of the Schneider Forberg Foundation in Munich and Crown Member of the Dutch Culture Council. Together with Dick Rijken he published the book "Media and Architecture". He is author of "SuperDutch", on recent architecture in the Netherlands (Thames & Hudson, Princeton Architectural Press, DVA and SUN, 2000) and published a monograph on B&K in 2003 and "Body & Globe", a collection of essays in 2004. He is the curator of Archilab 2004, the

international Architectural conference "The naked city" and member of the editorial board of GAM – Graz Architecture Magazine.

☐ ROSS LOVEGROVE

Ross Lovegrove was born 1958 in Cardiff, Wales. In the early 1980ies he worked as a designer for Frog Design in Germany on projects such as Walkmans for Sony, Computers for Apple, later he moved to Paris as a consultant to Knoll International. Invited to join the Atelier de Nimes along with Jean Nouvel and Philippe Starck. Returning to London in 1988 he has completed projects for, among others, British Airways, Kartell, Ceccotti, Cappellini, Idee, Moroso, Loom, Driade, Peuçeot, Apple, Connolly Leather, Olympus Cameras, Luceplan, Tag Heuer, Hackman, Alias, Herman Miller, Japan Airlines and Toyo Ito Architects. The winner of numerous international awards, his work has been extensively published and exhibited internationally including the Museum of Modern Art and the Guggenheim Museum, New York; Axis Centre Japan, Pompidou Centre, Paris and the Design Museum, London. Current projects in progress include the interior studies for the new Airbus A3XX (the largest commercial aircraft ever to be developed seating 680 passengers, due in service in 2005) and new lighting typologies for Luceplan.

☐ GREG LYNN FORM
GREG LYNN

Greg Lynn FORM has been at the cutting edge of design in the field of architecture when it comes to the use of computer-aided design. Greg Lynn FORM was established in 1994 in Hoboken, New Jersey and relocated to Venice, California in 1998 to take advantage of the knowledge and technology resources in both the manufacturing and entertainment industries of Southern California. The office is a design forward team that combines a unique specialization in exotic form and a creative ease and expertise with cutting edge design, manufacturing and construction techniques germane to the aeronautic, automobile and film industries of Southern California. Because of his early combination of degrees in philosophy and architecture, Greg Lynn has been involved in combining the realities of design and construction with the speculative, theoretical and experimental potentials of writing and teaching. He is the author of several books including most recently "intricacy" 2003. In the fall of 2002 he became Professor at the University of Applied Arts in Vienna, Austria. In addition, he is presently a Studio Professor at UCLA in Los Angeles and the Davenport Professor at Yale University.

☐ MVRDV
JAKOB VAN RIJS,
NATHALIE DE VRIES

Office for architecture and urbanism founded by Winy Maas, Jacob van Rijs and Natalie de Vries. Winy Maas, 1959, has worked as an architect/urban planner at: Bureau Bakker (Bleeker), Kuiper Compagnons (Rotterdam),

UNESCO (Nairobi), DHV (Amersfoort) and Rem Koolhaas' Office for Metropolitan Architecture (Rotterdam). Winy Maas lectures at AA London, Berlage Institute Amsterdam, Universities of Delft, Eindhoven, Berlin, Barcelona, Oslo and Vienna, at the Cooper Union New York and in Los Angeles, Chicago, Boston and Princeton. Jacob von Rijs, 1964, has worked as an architect at: Martinez Lapenas & Torres Arquitectos (Barcelona), Van Berkel en Bos (Amsterdam) and Rem Koolhaas' Office for Metropolitan Architecture (Rotterdam). Jacob von Rijs gives lectures at TU Delft, Architecture Academy Amsterdam and Rietveld Art Academy Amsterdam, AA London, Cooper Union New York, and also in Texas and Universities of Madrid and Barcelona. Nathalie de Vries, 1965, has worked as an architect at: Martinez Lapenas & Torres Arquitectos (Barcelona), D.J.V. Architects (Rotterdam) and Mecanoo Architects (Delft). Nathalie de Vries gives lectures at institutions all around the world. She has also been guest teacher at the Berlage Institute, the Academy of Building Arts in Arnhem and the Faculty of Architecture of the Technical University of Delft.

☐ OCEAN D – BOSTON, NEW YORK, LONDON
TOM VEREBES

ocean D is a multi-disciplinary design practice based in Boston, New York and London, integrating two nodes of the ocean network, ocean US and ocean UK. The partners and collaborators of ocean D have diverse backgrounds and skill-Sets that complement each other to form a broad-based design team. ocean D's profile and portfolio is posed at the next generation of design innovation, where collaborative research and development are fused with the commercial commissioning structure. ocean D eschews a singular category of product, but rather takes on a wide range of project-based design research projects. The suffix D encapsulates our expertise in the Interface of 3 synergetic fields of design practice: various scales of architectural practice; the emergent design category of interface design; and object design, from furniture to product design.

☐ OCEAN NORTH – ARCHITECTURE DESIGN RESEARCH
MICHAEL HENSEL, KIVI SOTAMAA

ocean NORTH is a design office with four associates in three European countries: Kivi & Tuuli Sotamaa in Helsinki, Michael Hensel in London and Birger Sevaldson in Oslo. The office focuses on projects, research and consulting in architecture, urban development, culture, and product and furniture design. OCEAN NORTH operates in the field of practical and experimental design and in research with the aim of identifying synergies in various spheres-from small-scale projects to architecture and urban planning. In order to attain this goal, ocean NORTH collaborates with a wide range of major experts in the various relevant disciplines.

☐ PETER OSWALD

Peter Oswald is the director of the art festival steirischer herbst. He studied music science, theatre science and art history at the University of Vienna where he also completed his PH.D. (doctoral thesis on the late work of Gustav Mahler). Peter Oswald has worked in various parts of the art field, he worked as music consultant for the Wiener Festwochen, he was head of the music department and later chief head of the television department at the ORF (Austrian Broadcast). From 1993-99 he was director of the Klangforum Wien and since 2000 he is director of steirischer herbst.

☐ PICHLER & TRAUPMANN
CHRISTOPH PICHLER, HANNES TRAUPMANN

Christoph Pichler, born in Vienna in 1964. 1983-1989 studies of architecture at the University of Applied Arts, Vienna, Prof. W. Holzbauer; studies of architecture at Graduate School of Design, Harvard University, USA; since 1992 lecturer at the Technical University of Vienna.
Hannes Traupmann, born in Güssing, Burgenland. 1977-1983 studies of theology at the Catholic Theological Faculty, University of Vienna; 1981-1987 studies of architecture at the University for Applied Arts, Vienna, Prof. W, Holzbauer; since 1992 collaboration with Christoph Pichler; 1995-1998 assistant at the University for Applied Arts, Vienna, Prof. W. Holzbauer; 1998 prize of the Association of Architects, Austria; since 1998 assistant at the University for Applied Arts, Vienna, Prof. Z. Hecker (Prof. Zaha Hadid since 2000); 2002

Architectural Award of Burgenland 2002. Pichler & Traupmann work on architecture as a transition in the ontological interplay of reality. Annulment and simultaneity are the yardstick and objective of almost all of their planned and built projects. The focus is on the performance of space and of the structures that generate space in the field of tension between apparent contradictions and opposites.

☐ PROPELLER Z
kabru

propeller z was established in 1994 and is based in Vienna, Austria. propeller z (Korkut Akkalay, kabru, Kriso Leinfellner, Philipp Tschofen, Carmen Wiederin) defines itself as a platform for space, content, material, form, and program research in all fields of two- or three-dimensional design. Its course will constantly evolve through the interaction of the various disciplines (as architecture, graphic design, exhibition design, set design, furniture design, concepts) and the input of the various members. propeller z develop their conceptual architecture out of productively dealing with function and programmatic constraints. Thus conceptual means their ability to connect parameters that both precede and are to result from the design process; this applies to their method of working in changing constellations as well as to decisions in the field of shifting formal possibilities. In doing this, the crossing of professional boundaries comes naturally. The members of propeller z are well trained in performing balancing acts between specialization and generalism, individualism and their identity as a group.

☐ ROGER RIEWE
(Organiser of space condition)

Roger Riewe studied architecture at the RWTH Aachen/Germany. Together with Florian Riegler he founded the architecture office "Riegler Riewe" 1987 in Graz, since 1997 the office has a branch in Cologne. Their major realizations include the Graz Airport, the Main Station Innsbruck and the Institutes for Information Technologies in Graz, currently the office is working on a restructuring of the Graz Trade Fair. Roger Riewe teaches world wide, he has given guest lectures at the Berlage Institute Rotterdam, RWTH Aachen, Technical university Prague, Caras-Workshop Syros, IAAS (Barcelona, Malberg, Venice), from 1999-2002 he was visiting professor at the ESARQ (UIC) Barcelona, Spain and since 2001 he is professor at the Institute for Architecture Technology, at the University of Technology in Graz, Austria. The work of Riegler Riewe has been exhibited and published internationally, most recently in the exhibition "TransModernity" in New York and Philadelphia in 2003. The office was part of the exhibition "New Trends of Architecture in Europe and Japan" 2002-04. In autumn 2004 a monograph of their work will be published by 2G. Roger Riewe is one of the editors in chief of GAM – Graz Architecture Magazine.

☐ SADAR VUGA ARHITEKTI
BOSTJAN VUGA

SVA was established 1996 in Ljubljana, after winning two competitions in summer 1996, which provided the financial background for its foundation. Its founders and proprietors are Jurij Sadar (1963) and Bostjan Vuga (1966). From its foundation on, SVA has employed 41 designers. Since 1996, SVA has produced 18 competition projects, 7 first-prize winning projects, and has obtained 41 project commissions. As SVA states, "production and communication are the means of achieving architectural effects and establishing an atmosphere", it has been appearing in technical and general media from the time of its foundation. SVA operates in an open and integral manner. For SVA, the development of new design techniques requires the inclusion of research in the design process. Only research can lead to novelty, the fresh and innovative architectural product. Innovation in architecture means the ability to produce new architectural effects that, through encounters, generate new 3D experiences for a user or perceiver. And this is what SVA strives for.

☐ PATRIK SCHUMACHER

Patrik Schumacher is director and project partner at Zaha Hadid Architects and co-director of the master degree programme "Design Research Laboratory" AADRL at the Architectural Association School of Architecture in London since 1996. He studied philosophy and architecture in Bonn, Stuttgart and London. He completed his Ph.D. at the Institute for Cultural Science at Klagenfurt University. He has been guest teacher at Columbia University in New York, Harvard University, Linz University and at the University of Illinois in Chicago. Since 2004 he is Professor at the Architecture Faculty at the University in Innsbruck, Austria.

□ SERVO
DAVID ERDMAN, MARCELYN GOW, ULRIKA KARLSSON, CHRIS PERRY

Established in 1999, servo's experimentation with emergent design, fabrication and interactive information technologies focuses on the complex interface of new media and architectural practice. With hubs in Los Angeles, New York, Stockholm, and Zurich, servo has held five solo exhibitions, taken part in five group exhibitions and have taught and lectured widely in both Europe and the US. Decentralized across four cities, three countries, and two continents, the collaborative borrows its name from an apparatus common in the field of cybernetics. servo motors translate digital code into machine processes. They act principally as enablers, allowing two discrete languages to converse and interact. Similarly, servo organizes, coordinates, and ultimately enables, on a variety of scales, new as well as existing relations between participants, technologies, disciplines, modes of production and communication, as well as a variety of cultural influences specific to each city in which it operates. To this extent servo resembles a kind of culture in formation, a microcommunity of participants, affiliate industries, technologies, and disciplines, which assume different organizational and formal characteristics over time and distance.

□ SOFTROOM
CHRISTOPHER BAGOT, OLIVER SALWAY

Softroom was founded in London in 1995 by Christopher Bagot, Dan Evans and Oliver Salway. The three first collaborated at the Bartlett School of Architecture, their entry for the International Cardiff Opera House Competition being one of those selected from the open field to join the invited stars in the final round. This success provided the impetus to build a practice around a core ability to develop bold and innovative architectural proposals and communicate them clearly through powerful and convincing imagery. An early collaboration with the magazine Wallpaper provided the opportunity to investigate visionary concepts in front of an international mass readership. In 1999, Softroom were invited to design a shelter in the Kielder forest, Northumberland. The resulting structure, the Kielder Belvedere, was awarded the Stephen Lawrence Prize and Royal Fine Art Commission-Jeu d'Esprit award. The RIBA jury commented, "We have never seen anything like this. It is rare to see such a genuinely original piece of architecture". Current commissions include the remodelling of the Devon Guild of craftsmen, improvements to the Royal Albert Hall and a public arts sculpture in North Swindon. Most recently they received winner in Best Industrial Design during the design weeks award 2004 for their suite design for Virgin Atlantic.

□ MICHAEL SPEAKS (Moderator)

Michael Speaks completed a Ph.D. at Duke University in 1993. He is the founding editor of Polygraph, and has been the Senior Editor at ANY magazine in New York, where he was also the Series Editor for "Writing Architecture" published by the MIT Press. Speaks has published and lectured internationally on art, architecture, urban design and scenario planning. A contributing editor for Architectural Record, Speaks also serves on the senior editorial advisory board of A+U (Japan) and Archis (The Netherlands), and on the advisory board of the Storefront for Art and Architecture in New York City. Currently Director of the Metropolitan Research and Design Post Graduate Program at the Southern California Institute of Architecture in Los Angeles, Speaks also heads the Los Angeles-based urban research group, BIG SOFT ORANGE.

□ BRETT STEELE (Moderator)

Brett Steele directs, with Patrik Schumacher, the AADRL Design Research Lab at the Architectural Association School of Architecture.
The AADRL is a sixteen-month M.Arch course. "Transistory Urbanism", on the Brand.Space studios of the AADRL was recently published in Trans_Urbanism. Other recent articles on the AADRL have appeared in Arch+, Archis, Harvard Design Magazine, Daidalos, and AA Files. He is the editor of "RAMTV [Negotiate My Boundary!]", "Corporate Fields: Machinic Office Environments" (forthcoming) and founding editor with Andrew Benjamin of Res_arch, a new international journal of

architectural ideas that will launch in spring 2003. He is currently completing "Brand.Space: aRchitecture v. 2.0."

☐ the next ENTERprise
ERNST J. FUCHS,
MARIE THERESE
HARNONCOURT

Ernst J. Fuchs and Marie Therese Harnoncourt founded the next ENTERprise-architects in 2000 in Vienna. They are both graduates of the University of Applied Arts in Vienna, and have been working together since the early 1990s. During this period they mainly worked in collaboration with Florian Haydn as the Poor Boy's Enterprise. As authors of artistic and experimental installations (Hirnsegel No. 7, 1995, Stadtwind 2000, vanishing space 2000) and demanding architectural works (House Zirl, 1997, underground pool 2001, public pool Kaltern 2002, House Fidesser / Retz 2003), these two Viennese architects single out the importance of form (for which they eschew any kind of preconception) solely by validating the complex processes of which it is the product. For them, the work involved in a project proceeds above all, through a gradual updating of a specific and original procedure capable of "fertilizing" all the erratic and fragmentary data provided, unselectively, by the Situation. This is a procedure capable of progressively organizing these primary conditions within a conscious development, and within a formal and conceptual formulation. This architecture, which is available to itself, is offered, in all its complexity, for the user.

☐ UN STUDIO
BEN VAN BERKEL

Ben van Berkel studied at the Rietveld Academy in Amsterdam and the Architectural Association in London. Together with Caroline Bos he founded the Van Berkel & Bos architectural office in Amsterdam (1988). Their Erasmus Bridge in Rotterdam, Valkhof Museum in Nijmegen and Mobius House are just three examples taken from a large and varied body of work. In 1998 Van Berkel and Bos explicitly chose to steer their architectural practice in a new direction and Set up UN Studio. This network of researchers and specialists in architecture, urban development and infrastructure creates perceptive projects that seamlessly weld together brief, construction, infrastructure, circulation, form and space. UN Studio is currently completing the New Mercedes Benz Museum in Stuttgart and the La Defense Offices in Almere. Besides his architectural work, Ben van Berkel lectures at several architectural schools around the world and participates, with his writings, in international debates on architecture and new media. Recent publications are "UNFold" (Nai publishers 2002, Rotterdam) and "MOVE" (UN Studio and Goose Press) Amsterdam 1999. Since 2001 Ben van Berkel is dean of the architecture class at the Städelschule in Frankfurt (Germany).

☐ VEECH.MEDIA.ARCHITECTURE
STUART VEECH,
MASCHA VEECH-KOSMATSCHOF

veech.media.architecture was founded in 1993 in Vienna as an interdisciplinary unit of architects, media designers and artists specialized in architectural design, virtual technology, and art installations. Stuart A. Veech, born in Chicago, USA, received a diploma in Urban Design from the University of Cincinnati, USA and studied at the Architectural Association, London. Since 1998, lecturer at the Technical University of Vienna, Department of Architecture, Prof. William Alsop. Mascha Veech-Kosmatschof, born in Moscow, Russia, studied at the University of Applied Arts, Vienna, with Prof. Wilhelm Holzbauer and at the Architectural Association, London, with Jan Kaplicky, Ron Herron, and Zaha Hadid, receiving an AA Diploma in 1991. Since 2001, teaching assistant at the University of Applied Art, Vienna, Prof. Zaha Hadid.

WE WOULD LIKE TO THANK FOR THEIR SUPPORT IN PRODUCING THIS PUBLICATION:

steirisc[:her:]bst

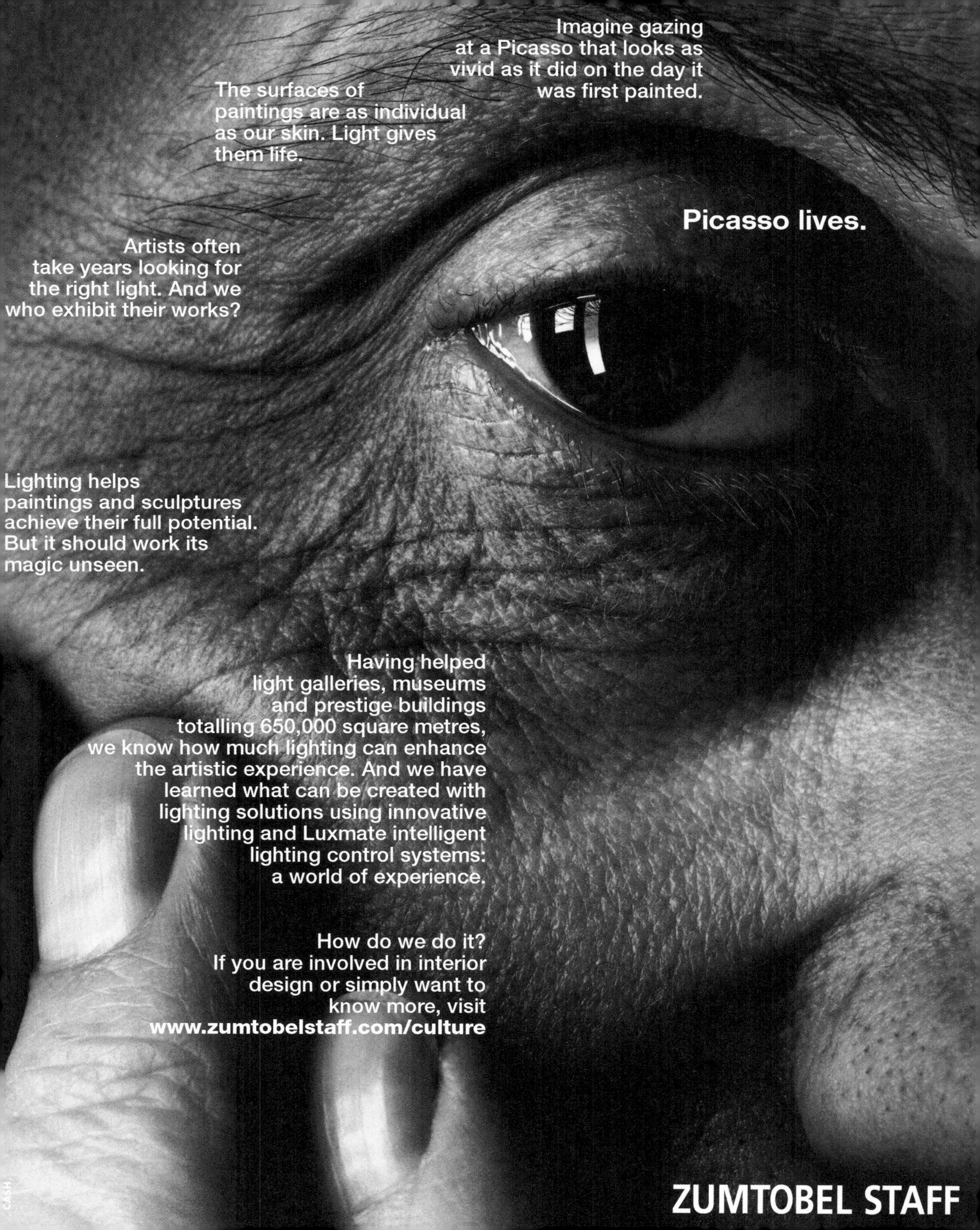

Imagine gazing
at a Picasso that looks as
vivid as it did on the day it
was first painted.

The surfaces of
paintings are as individual
as our skin. Light gives
them life.

Picasso lives.

Artists often
take years looking for
the right light. And we
who exhibit their works?

Lighting helps
paintings and sculptures
achieve their full potential.
But it should work its
magic unseen.

Having helped
light galleries, museums
and prestige buildings
totalling 650,000 square metres,
we know how much lighting can enhance
the artistic experience. And we have
learned what can be created with
lighting solutions using innovative
lighting and Luxmate intelligent
lighting control systems:
a world of experience.

How do we do it?
If you are involved in interior
design or simply want to
know more, visit
www.zumtobelstaff.com/culture

ZUMTOBEL STAFF

space condition

Editor
Roger Riewe

Editor in Chief
Roger Riewe
supported by Eva Grubbauer and Eva Guttmann

Graphic Design
Atelier Neubacher, Graz

Printing
Holzhausen Druck & Medien GmbH, Wien
Printed on acid-free and chlorine-free bleached paper

Translations
Y-plus – Susanne Baumann

Proof-reading
Margarette Stiehler

Printing
Holzhausen Druck & Medien GmbH, Wien

Photo credits
steirischer herbst

Address
Roger Riewe
Institute for Architecture Technology
Graz University of Technology
Rechbauerstrasse 12
A 8010 Graz
Austria
F: 0043 316 873 6301
Riewe@at.tugraz.at

Sponsors
Graz University of Technology, Land Steiermark, steirischer herbst, Zumtobel, Bene, Armstrong DLW, Schüco-Alu-König

Copyright
2005 Springer-Verlag/Wien and the authors
Printed in Austria
Springer-Verlag/Wien is part of Springer
Science+Business Media
springeronline.com

Printed on acid-free and chlorine-free bleached paper
SPIN: 10974322

Bibliografische Information der Deutschen Bibliothek.
Die Deutsche Bibliothek verzeichnet diese Publikation in der Deutschen Nationalbibliografie; detaillierte Daten sind im Internet über http://dnb.ddb.de abrufbar.

With numerous (partly coloured) Figures

ISBN 3-211-20634-5

□ **space condition**
International Architecture Symposium
25. 10. 2002, Graz University of Technology

□ Organized by Graz University of Technology,
Faculty of Architecture in co-production with
steirischer herbst

□ Concept
Roger Riewe

□ Organization
Christian Kronaus

□ Graphic design
Gernot Kupfer

□ Multimedia
**Johann Grabner, Herwig Baumgartner
Elisabeth Nöst-Kahlen**

□ Media support
Peter Javurek

□ Public Relations
Günter Koberg

□ Logistics
Manuel Lebeda

□ Interviews
**Eva Grubbauer, Anja Jonkhans
Elisabeth Nöst-Kahlen, Heywon Seo**

□ Staff
Institute for Architecture Technology

□ **space condition** was organized within the context
of the "Latent Utopias" exhibition curated by
Patrik Schumacher and Zaha Hadid for steirischer
herbst 2002/2003. For the exhibition a catalogue
with the same title was published by Springer Verlag
publishers, Vienna.

Imprint